PAUL
AND THE
CHRISTIAN
WOMAN

PAUL
AND THE
CHRISTIAN
WOMAN

BRENDAN BYRNE SJ

Foreword by
Francis J. Moloney sdb

THE LITURGICAL PRESS
Collegeville, Minnesota

Cover design by Br. Joshua Jeide, O.S.B.

Printed in the United States of America.

1	2	3	4	5	6	7	8	9

Library of Congress Cataloging-in-Publication Data

Byrne, Brendan, S.J.
    Paul and the Christian woman / Brendan Byrne ; foreword by Francis J. Moloney.
        p. cm.
    Bibliography: p.
    Includes index.
    ISBN 0-8146-1846-4
    1. Women in the Bible. 2. Bible. N.T. Epistles of Paul—Criticism, interpretation, etc. 3. Paul, the Apostle, Saint—Views on women. I. Title.
BS2655.W5B97   1989   89-36071
227'.06'082—dc20   CIP

For **Pamela Foulkes,**
whose gentle encouragement and wise advice
have accompanied this project
from the beginning

Foreword

There are many issues which face sincere followers of Jesus in these last decades of the second Christian millenium. The person and the role of the Christian woman is one of the more urgent of these concerns. Within the wider setting of the women's movement, the struggle of Christian women to stand equal with men before God is a nagging thorn in the side of a Church whose authority and ministry has become over-masculine. This struggle will not 'go away' if it is ignored long enough. The words of Gamaliel I to the Jerusalem Council leap to mind: 'If this plan or undertaking is merely human, it will fail; but if it is of God, you will not be able to overthrow them. You might even be found opposing God!' (Acts 5:38-39).

In the uniquely Christian process of discernment which both women and men must undertake in the Churches (as it is not only men who prefer a male-directed Church!), a crucial place must be given to the Word of God. It is here that we are in touch with the inspired written beginnings of the Christian tradition. My own understanding of the earliest days of the Christian phenomenon is that Jesus of Nazareth unleashed an incredible 'newness' into the balance of relationships between women and men and, consequently, between woman, man and God. This can be traced through a careful and critical reading of the Gospel narratives about Jesus' contacts with women and his teachings in which the role of woman is crucial. I was delighted to see that Brendan Byrne shares my understanding.

What, however, are we to make of the next stop as Christian tradition developed? What are we to make of the first Christian preacher-writer: Paul of Tarsus? Those of us whose knowledge of Paul comes from a nodding acquaintance . . . and not from a first-hand contact with *all* his correspondence . . . will probably feel that he is a stern advocate of woman's secondary role in Christian ministry (1 Cor 11:2-16; 14:34-35), and subordinate role within Christian marriage (1 Cor 7:32-35).

We are about to be surprised. Brendan Byrne's study has, to my mind, set the issue straight. While there have been numerous detailed studies of the various difficult passages from Paul, there has been no single study devoted wholly to the Pauline and post-Pauline material. Brendan Byrne's work guides the reader through all the difficult texts with a sure and expert hand.

The reader may have been surprised to notice that the most troublesome passages, mentioned above, all come from 1 Corinthians. I wonder why? You will find the answers in the work which follows. This book begins where all study of Paul must begin: with the Apostle's insistence that 'in Christ' all divisions and separations accepted as 'normal' by the religions and culture of his time must not be allowed to remain (see Gal 3:26-28). Only on the basis of this primary assertion of Paul is it legitimate to study the rest of his developing thought on this urgent question.

Because of its starting point, this book is 'right-headed'. Fr Byrne does not set out to show that Paul must be supportive of our modern issue. On the contrary, we will see there are places where Paul seems to pay a price for pastoral effectiveness which we may judge too high. But Paul must be allowed to be Paul. It is important that we recognise in the writings of this pastor from the first decades of the Christian story what is ultimately a 'word of life' for us, but the process needed to arrive at such a recognition can be delicate. This too has been beautifully handled for you in the work which you are about to read.

It often strikes me that the most serious issue that the contemporary Church must face in its teaching ministry is the communication of the essentially historical nature of God's revelation to us. Fortunately, the Christian faith did not begin with its dogmas and practices already clearly indicated in some sort of definitive text. The attempts to write such texts have only come at a later stage!

The relationships between women and men, and the consequent relationship which exists between women and men who must stand equal before God, has only been properly lived by one person in our history: Jesus of Nazareth. Paul saw this challenge, and attempted to place it at the heart of his message. Have the few pastoral concessions which he has been forced to make merited him the accusation of being the male chauvinist of the New Testament? The book you are about to read will raise exactly that question . . . and offer an honest solution.

Francis J. Moloney, S.D.B.
Salesian Theological College
Oakleigh 3166, Australia

Contents

List of Abbreviations

BAG Bauer, W., Arndt, W.F., and Gingrich, F.W., *A Greek English Lexicon of the New Testament and Other Early Christian Literature*, Chicago: University of Chicago, 1957.

BDF Blass, F., Debrunner, R. and Funk, R.W., *A Grammar of the New Testament and Other Early Christian Literature*, Chicago: University of Chicago, 1961.

BETL Bibliotheca ephemeridum theologicarum lovanensium.

BTB *Biblical Theology Bulletin.*

BZ *Biblische Zeitschrift.*

CBQ *Catholic Biblical Quarterly.*

EvQ *Evangelical Quarterly.*

HDR Harvard Dissertations in Religion.

HR *History of Religions.*

ICC International Critical Commentary.

IDBSupp Supplementary Volume to G.A. Buttrick (ed.) *Interpreter's Dictionary of the Bible*, Nashville: Abingdon, 1976.

JAAR *Journal of the American Academy of Religion.*

JahrAntChrist *Jahrbuch für Antike und Christentum.*

JBC Brown, R.E. et. al. (eds.), *The Jerome Biblical Commentary*, 2 vols., Englewood Cliffs, NJ: Prentice-Hall, 1968.

JBL *Journal of Biblical Literature.*

JSNT *Journal for the Study of the New Testament.*

LSJ Liddell, H.G., Scott, R., *A Greek-English Lexicon*, rev. by H.S. Jones with a *Supplement*, 9th ed.; Oxford: Clarendon, 1940.

NTS *New Testament Studies.*

RSR *Religious Studies Review.*

RSV *Revised Standard Version.*

SBLDS Society of Biblical Literature Dissertation Series.

SBLMS	Society of Biblical Literature Monograph Series.
ScEs	*Science et esprit.*
SVTP	Studia in Veteris Testamenti pseudepigrapha.
TDNT	Kittel, G. and Friedrich, G. (eds.), *Theological Dictionary of the New Testament*, 10 vols., Grand Rapids: Eerdmans, 1964-76.
TQ	*Theologische Quartalschrift.*
TS	*Theological Studies.*
USQR	*Union Seminary Quarterly Review.*
WTJ	*Westminster Theological Journal.*
ZNW	*Zeitschrift für die neutestamentliche Wissenschaft.*

Introduction

In any discussion of woman's place in the life and ministry of the Church the writings of Paul bulk large. It is hardly an exaggeration to say that the Pauline literature in the New Testament has formed the battleground upon which women's issues in the Church have been contested. Paul is cited as authority for keeping women 'silent' in the assembly, for their exclusion from ministry. He is also cited, as 'the one clear voice in the New Testament asserting the freedom and equality of women in the ... community'.[1]

Most women aspiring to a more equal role in the Church would, I suspect, take some convincing about Paul's being an ally in the cause. They might not go as far as George Bernard Shaw and describe Paul as 'the eternal enemy of woman'.[2] But they find the positive messages in his writings far outweighed by others that seem to put women firmly in their place — an inferior, subordinate place. Paul, if not constantly hostile, is at least inconsistent in the matter and seems to lack in the long run the courage of his earlier convictions.

Paul's statements about women do not stand at the centre of his writings. They are hardly representative of him at his best. For a long time when teaching and speaking about Paul I tended to skirt them and take up what to my view were the more central, more creative areas.

It has, however, proved impossible to continue in this way. My experience has been that, in speaking and lecturing on Paul, as far as a good half of the audience is concerned, there is one question that stands at the forefront of consciousness: 'Wasn't Paul a misogynist?', 'Didn't he have it in for women?' Once the discussion begins, taking up the question of Paul's attitude to women is not negotiable. Today this issue *is* central. Any attempt to discuss or communicate Paul's magnificent vision of a world coming to full humanity in Christ is doomed to frustration as long as one half of the human race seems to be left behind.

My writing of this book arises, then, immediately out of this experience when speaking and lecturing on Paul. I wish to respond to many requests to lay out the relevant material and offer some critical assessment. Not that the Pauline material has not already received ample discussion both in technical and popular literature. However, such discussion of Paul tends to be either scattered across a large range of journals or else forms simply a section of a monograph offering a wider survey – 'Woman in the New Testament', or the like. At present I am not aware of any monograph devoted entirely to the Pauline literature readily available in English.

The Pauline material on woman does, of course, feature prominently in E. Schüssler Fiorenza's monumental study, *In Memory of Her: A Feminist Theological Reconstruction of Christian Origins.*[3] To a very large degree, as will readily become apparent, throughout the present study I am in debt to and dialogue with this groundbreaking work. I know of no survey or discussion where the Pauline material receives such sustained and comprehensive critical discussion as in the latter part of *In Memory of Her.* Using a feminist critical model of interpretation ('feminist hermeneutic of suspicion') Professor Fiorenza aims to reconstruct early Christian history as women's history, to recover the traces of the original discipleship of equals and the partnership in mission that flowed from it, to chart the gradual displacement of women's leadership under the influence of tendencies towards male dominance ('androcentric tendencies') that shape virtually the entire written record contained in the New Testament. The hope is not merely to restore women's stories to early Christian history but to allow the recovery of the egalitarian witness in the New Testament to spark anew a nonpatriarchal Christian vision and praxis.[4]

Those who have worked closely through the Pauline section of *In Memory of Her* may well find the present study unnecessary and less satisfying. My aim, however, is somewhat different. I do not propose to use the Pauline material to reconstruct a history of woman's place in early Christianity. My intention is to study the texts concerning women in their contexts and to try to assess as accurately as possible their meaning and purpose in their original setting. I hope to indicate the circumstances in the communities which gave rise to Paul's statements and which may account for whatever development in his thought appears to take place. The chief focus lies upon the mind of Paul and the relating of his statements on women to his overall sense of Christian status and mission.

Undertaking this survey as a man, I am well aware that a woman pursuing the same enquiry might proceed in a rather different way and come to somewhat variant conclusions. That in a sense is what Elisabeth Schüssler Fiorenza has done.[5] My understanding of Paul has been shaped and constantly challenged by women whom I have taught and who have taught me. Hopefully some of their insight colours this enquiry. But in the end it remains a man's view of Paul, doubtless in need of complementing from another point of view. It is not offered, then, as the last word or as a totally adequate survey of the question. It is simply the enquiry of one male Pauline scholar into the material as he sees it.

At this point it may help to indicate the texts in Pauline literature which must come up in the discussion. The starting point has always been and doubtless will continue to be the strikingly egalitarian statement of Christian existence to be found in Gal 3:27-28:

[27] For as many of you as were baptized into Christ have put on Christ:
[28] there is neither Jew nor Greek
there is neither slave nor free
there is neither male and female.

Next there arises the attitude to women implicit in Paul's long response to questions on marriage and celibacy in 1 Corinthians 7, followed shortly after in the same letter by the lengthy discussion of women's attire when praying and prophesying in the Christian assembly, 1 Cor 11:2-16. Finally in 1 Corinthians there is the sharp injunction appearing in chapter 14 that women are to be silent in the assembly and ask questions of their husbands at home, 1 Cor 14:33-36. In Col 3:18 we find an injunction to wives to be subject to their husbands, something which finds development and deeper theological grounding in Eph 5:21-33. There is a scatter of references to women in the Pastoral letters (1 Tim 2:9-15; 3:11; 5:3-16; 2 Tim 3:6-7; Tit 2:3-6). Also, the discussion must take account of references to women as co-workers of Paul, which occur, chiefly in greetings, in the earlier letters.

The debate concerning Paul's attitude towards women intensified in the early 1970s as the feminist movement began to make an impact upon New Testament studies. Alongside bitter attacks upon the influence of Paul, there appeared numerous studies seeking to improve his feminist credentials. Virtually all recognise the uniquely egalitarian tenor of the statement in Gal 3:27-28. The question is whether Paul in subsequent writings betrayed or backed away from the egalitarian ideal expressed in the third member of v. 28.[6]

Most critical scholars, for reasons which will be discussed later, tend to regard the Pastoral Letters (1-2 Timothy, Titus) and Ephesians as not the product of Paul but as compositions stemming from a later period. A somewhat reduced number, though still a majority, of scholars would place Colossians in the same category. Thus in questing for the attitude of Paul himself they exclude consideration of these letters and turn only to the earlier material. But even here interpreters go different ways.

The elimination of the Deutero-Pauline material makes the task of those seeking to find a positive attitude emerging from Paul much easier. But still there remain two problematic passages in 1 Corinthians: the statement about woman's attire in 11:2-16 and the injunction to silence in the assembly in 14:33-36. A considerable number of scholars, for reasons which we shall later discuss, regard the latter passage as an interpolation into the text of 1 Corinthians by a later writer having much affinity with the author of the Pastoral letters. A few scholars take the same position with regard to the more lengthy statement about women's attire in chapter 11.[7] But this view has not won general acceptance.

Hence the judgment as to whether Paul did or did not decline from the egalitarian ideal expressed in Gal 3:28 tends to be decided according to the interpretation one places upon 1 Cor 11:2-16. If an interpretation that is thoroughly positive to women can be drawn from this passage, as many recent interpreters have claimed, then the issue concerning Paul's attitude to women is largely won for the positive sense. If, on the contrary, the more traditional, subordinationist view prevails, then Paul tends to be seen as the initiator of the trend to the more patriarchal, androcentric tendency of the later New Testament texts. There is a sense, then, in which the interpretation of 1 Cor 11:2-16 stands at the centre of any enquiry into the issue before us. Certainly that will be reflected in the present study.

Though avowedly sympathetic to Paul, my conscious aim is not that of seeking to cull an entirely positive view of women from his writings. Nor do I want to defend him at all costs. Feminist writers have rightly deplored the efforts of Pauline scholars who give the appearance of being more concerned about the reputation of an apostle long dead than about the effects of his writings upon the treatment given to women in religious circles today.[8] Paul has long since gained his desire 'to depart and be with Christ' (Phil 1:23). What is crucial today is the way his writings are interpreted and employed within the Church.

Yet, while it is true that modern interpretation of Paul cannot be confined to his original meaning, the attempt to reach for that meaning, if successful, may be liberating in its own right. Certainly, it must form the starting point for a valid interpretation. If we can search for and discover what Paul's attitude may have been and accept it, palatable or unpalatable, then we have a basis for the separate, second task of enquiring after the meaning and proper employment of these texts today.

My procedure will be to take the relevant passages one by one, beginning with the statement in Gal 3:28. As I have indicated above, the centrepiece of the enquiry will be to see what becomes of the ideal expressed there in the practical application of the gospel to be found in 1 Corinthians — specifically 1 Corinthians 7, 11 and 14. In each case I will not focus narrowly upon the text in question, but attempt to set it in its broader context so that the question about women emerges from within a wider vision of Paul's theology. There follows a chapter on the hints contained in various places of the involvement of women as Paul's co-workers. As stated above, I do not regard the later letters — Colossians, Ephesians and the Pastorals — as written by Paul himself. Yet since it is the material in these writings that so widely moulds the perception of Paul's views on women, the study would not be complete if they were not reviewed. In particular, it is helpful, I feel, to give some consideration to the reasons that led later generations to modify the original insights and ideals.

The immediate origins of this book lie in a series of three evening lectures given to the Melbourne Scripture Seminar in September 1986. Needless to say, the project has greatly expanded upon the content of those three lectures. My original intention was to write a short popular account of the topic, more or less confined to a resume of what scholars were presently saying and writing on Paul. Almost from the start, however, it became clear that I could not simply present opinions with which I found myself in disagreement, nor could I register disagreement without stating the reasons for and against. I found myself composing, then, a somewhat more scholarly account than originally intended.

I can only hope that this development will not limit the more popular appeal of this book. To this end I have tried to restrict detailed dialogue with scholarly opinion to the notes. I have also attempted to explain any technical terminology that has had to be included in the text.

But my experience in popular presentation has been that general audiences can appreciate the reasons for positions and like to be told of them, provided they can be clearly explained; they do not want to be patronised by 'canned' solutions. A study which bears upon an issue of such central concern for the Church today must try to give each adult Christian the wherewithal to make as informed and honest a judgment as possible. I can only hope that the present work will help to that end — even if entrance into the mind and world of Paul will demand, as it always does, no little effort of mind and will.

---

[1] Robin Scroggs, 'Paul and the Eschatological Woman', *JAAR* 40 (1972) 283-303, esp. p.302.

[2] Cited E. Pagels, 'Paul and Women: A Response to Recent Discussion', *JAAR* 42 (1974) 543-49, esp. p. 543.

[3] New York: Crossroad, 1983; London: SCM, 1983.

[4] The hermeneutical discussion makes up the first third of the work, pp. xiii-xxxv, 1-95. For the summary above see esp. pp. xiv-xvi, 56.

[5] While saying this, I find quite unreasonable the judgement of A. Padgett concerning *In Memory of Her*: 'There is in this book a subtle thematic which, in almost every case, interprets the Pauline corpus in as chauvinistic a manner as possible' ('Feminism in First Corinthians: A Dialogue with Elisabeth Schüssler Fiorenza', *EvQ* 58 [1986] 121-32, see p. 132).

[6] For a thorough review of positions taken on this issue, along with a comprehensive bibliography, see D. R. MacDonald, *There is No Male and Female* (HDR 20; Philadelphia: Fortress, 1986) 2-5.

[7] For this view see esp. W. O. Walker, Jr., '1 Corinthians 11:2-16 and Paul's Views Regarding Women', *JBL* 94 (1975) 94-100; idem, 'The "Theology of Woman's Place" and the "Paulinist" Tradition', *Semeia* 28 (1983) 101-12; L. Cope, '1 Cor. 11,2-16: One Step Further', *JBL* 97 (1978) 435-36; G. W. Trompf, 'On Attitudes toward Women in Paul and Paulinist Literature', *CBQ* 42 (1980) 196-215.

[8] Cf. the citations in R. Scroggs, 'Paul and the Eschatological Woman Revisited', *JAAR* 42 (1974) 532-37, see esp. 532-33.

Chapter 1

'There is No Male and Female':
Galatians 3:28

The recipients of the Letter to the Galatians were Gentile Christians, evangelised by Paul in the course of his missionary activity in central Asia Minor (cf. Acts 16:6; 18:23). Since his successful winning of them to the law-free gospel which he proclaimed to the Gentiles, they had come under the influence of other Christian preachers who placed more stress on the Jewish legacy. Contrary to Paul's instruction, these sought to persuade the new Galatian converts that to gain salvation they must adopt circumcision and the commitment to the Jewish law which it implied. Paul, convinced that the essence of the gospel was at stake, writes in burning indignation to counter this deviation and assure the Galatians that the law-free preaching which they received, and to which they must adhere, is the only true form of the gospel for them as Gentiles.

In his defence of the original preaching, Paul first takes a somewhat autobiographical tack. He points to key incidents in his Christian career to re-establish his credentials as a genuine apostle, directly commissioned by the risen Lord and with a specific brief for the conversion of the Gentiles (Gal 1:16-17). Not only does he have this status quite independently of the authorities in Jerusalem (2:13-24), but the leading trio — Peter, James and John (Paul calls them 'the pillars') — have formally acknowledged his right to proclaim to Gentiles this law-free gospel (2:1-10). Then, as the centre-piece of the entire letter, he deploys a long argument interweaving both Scriptural exegesis and the experience of the Spirit (3:1 — 5:1).

The experience of the Spirit is crucial for Paul, since the Spirit is the eschatological gift *par excellence*. To have received the Spirit is to have entered into the New Age, to have passed from the old situation of slavery and fear to the freedom and intimacy that marks a genuinely filial relationship to God. To want to submit, through circumcision, to the yoke of the law means going back to the Old

1

Age, to a situation of religious slavery and fear which was never meant for them as Gentiles and which would correspond to their former subservience to idols and false gods (4:9-11). Above all, it would annul the redemptive work of Christ, upon whom the passage from the Old Age to the New hinges (2:21).

So Paul appeals directly to the experience of the Galatians, to the experience of the Spirit which they received when they gave an assent in faith to the original preaching of the gospel (3:1-5). It is through living out this life in the Spirit that they are being readied for the fullness of life and humanity yet to come.

But Paul does not simply remind the Galatians that they have received the Spirit through faith. He is at pains to show that this was always the way God had meant it to be. He shows this by going to Scripture, the key indicator of God's intent for the final age. Above all, he goes to the story of Abraham because, along with all other Jews, he believed that it was in the career of Abraham, and especially in the promises made to him by God, that the whole pattern of future salvation was set out. So Paul indicates God's will for the community by reading Scripture in the light of the experience of the Spirit – a very early and normative instance of Christian discernment.

Abraham in Galatians 3: the working of the promise

At the heart of his scriptural argument in Galatians 3 Paul sets up a great antithesis between the dispensation of the law, including the rite of circumcision, and the promise made to Abraham. God drew Abraham into right relationship with himself (he 'justified' him) solely on the basis of his faith and God further promised that he and all his descendants (lit. 'his seed' [sing.]) would be 'blessed' on the same basis. In this 'blessing' Paul, following a Jewish tradition, sees contained the whole content of salvation, including the gift of the Spirit.[1] The 'blessing' forges an arc of grace that springs from God's original word to Abraham right across to those who in Christ are the faith-people of the New Age. In between comes the law given in mediated fashion to Moses. But this 'Johnny-come-lately' on the scene has no power in Paul's eyes to disturb the arc of salvation established on the basis of faith. The law, with its precept of circumcision, was given for a wholly different purpose and was meant for the Jews only. Even for them it was not to provide a means of justification; it was to serve as a kind of 'pedagogue', leading to faith (3:21-25).

To show that the law has no role in the workings of the promise, Paul takes up the image of a will or testament which a person makes to determine inheritance (3:15-17). He applies this to God's disposition and promise as spoken to Abraham. God made the promise to Abraham 'and to his seed'. In the Greek version of the Old Testament the word 'seed', *sperma*, is collective in sense (= 'your descendants') but singular in construction. Upon this small grammatical point Paul constructs an argument quite arbitrary to modern readers but typical of the scriptural interpretation of his own day. From the singular usage of 'seed' he argues (3:16) that the intended beneficiary of the promise, as descendant or 'seed' of Abraham, was primarily and *per se* a single person, namely Christ. Others can come under the scope of the promise only through him. So, just as no one can add to a will once it has been ratified or write in new conditions, so the Law, coming on the scene so much later, cannot alter this fundamental disposition of God; it cannot impose extra or rival conditions of inheriting the promise, such as the way of circumcision; it cannot give entrance to the promise in any way that bypasses the sole primary heir: Christ.

So for Paul the only way you come under the saving scope of the promise is by intimate association with Christ. That association, begun by faith and cemented in the rite of baptism, is a very radical process in which one 'dies' in terms of one's old, individual 'ego' and literally 'enters' the Risen Christ as a personal, corporate sphere of salvation. The divisive categories that belonged to the old existence and defined it − Jew over against Greek (Gentile), slave against free, male against female − are cast aside as one simply takes on the persona of Christ and the new eschatological existence that goes with it.

Paul's description of the process in v. 26 in terms of 'putting on' Christ evokes the image of the Greek drama where actors adopted the persona of the character they were playing by donning a totally enveloping costume. So complete was the covering that the original identity of the actor totally disappeared and all the audience saw was the character portrayed. For Paul this is what happens when you 'enter' the 'one seed', Christ, in order to come under the scope of the promise. You die to the old existence, with its allegiances and obligations. You abandon a purely individual quest for salvation and throw yourself upon the grace offered communally in the 'one seed', Christ. 'In' him you enter the New Age. You receive the promised Spirit and cry out to God with the intimate and trusting address characteristic of Jesus: *'Abba,* Father' (4:6).

'Neither Male and Female ...': the baptismal formula

It is in this context of oneness in Christ in order to inherit the promise that there occurs the reference to 'no longer male and female' that is our principal concern. Let us set out the passage in full:

> [26] For you are all sons of God through faith, in Christ Jesus.
> [27] For as many of you as were baptized into Christ have put on Christ:
> > [28] there is neither *Jew* nor *Greek*
> > there is neither *slave* nor *free*
> > there is neither *male* and *female*
> > For you are all one person in Christ Jesus.
> [29] And if you belong to Christ in this way,
> then you are seed of Abraham, heirs according to the promise.

When we attend to the structure and wider context of this passage it soon becomes clear that Paul's main concern is not to teach the abolition of distinctions (Jew/Greek; slave/free; etc.) in the community. The statement about the overcoming of distinctions is not central but rather stands at the service of the more basic intent, which is to emphasise oneness. Since believers make up one person in the whole Christ, since they are included thereby in the '(one) seed of Abraham', they share in his inheritance of the promise. They are in this sense 'sons of God' (v. 26), that is, those destined to inherit the full blessings of salvation in the New Age. In the gift of the Spirit they already have a foretaste of that New Age (4:6-7). The law, with its claims and threats and slavery, is for them totally irrelevant and *passé.*

But even if the statement in v. 28 about the abolition of distinctions stands at the service of a somewhat different concern, it bears closer examination in its own right. In both content and symmetry it has some formal parallels in other places in Pauline literature. In 1 Cor 12:12-13 we read:

> [12] For just as the body is one and has many members, and all the members of the body, though many, are one body, so it is with the Christ:

¹³ for by one Spirit we were all baptized into one body —
whether   *Jew* or *Greeks*
          slaves or *free* —
          and all were made to drink of the one Spirit.

Here we meet two of the pairs that feature in Gal 3:28. But the third — 'male and female' — is missing. The significance of this omission in 1 Corinthians I shall take up later. For the present let us note other parallel features. The focus on the Spirit is more explicit here than in the Galatians passage. But there is the same emphasis on oneness and specifically on oneness in the person of 'the Christ', with Paul's 'body of Christ' image for the Christian community coming explicitly to the fore.

As we shall also consider later, the letter to the Colossians is now widely regarded as not directly composed by Paul. But it undoubtably reflects and echoes much of his thinking. In the exhortatory portion that begins in chapter 3 we read,

^{9b} Having put off the old man with his practices and
¹⁰ having put on the new, the one that is being renewed in knowledge after the image of his Creator,
¹¹ where there is neither
          Greek nor *Jew*,
          circumcision nor *uncircumcision*,
          barbarian or *Scythian*,
          slave or *free*
          but Christ is all in all.

Here we meet again the same two categories as in 1 Cor 12:13 (the first two of Gal 3:28), with some augmentation between them. Also, at the end, there is the same reference to the total all-inclusive person of Christ. A significant new feature, however, is the explicit reference to the creation of human beings according to Gen 1:26-27. The new Christian existence is pictured as being modelled on Christ, who as 'Last Adam' fulfils humankind's original destiny of being created in the image of God (Gen 1:26-27).

Explicit allusions to 'new creation' are to be found in other Pauline texts. These speak of the new communal existence in Christ in terms highly reminiscent of the passages we have been considering. So, for example, 2 Cor 5:17:

Therefore, if anyone is in Christ, he is a *new creation*: the old has passed away, the new has come.

And Gal 6:15:

> For neither circumcision counts for anything, nor the lack of it, but behold a new creation!

These parallels, plus a significant clue occurring in Gal 3:28 itself, suggest that the idea of 'new creation' is central to all these passages.

The clue in the case of Gal 3:28 consists in the fact that whereas the first two pairs, 'Jew and Greek, slave and free' are joined disjunctively ('neither . . . nor . . .'), the final pair, reads 'male *and* female'. Controlling the rather awkward change would seem to be the language of the creation account in Gen 1:26-27. In other words, what is being described here is the creation 'in Christ' of a new humanity, a humanity for the New Age, where the divisions and distinctions significant in the Old Age are simply dissolved in the all-embracing corporate existence in Christ. What God is doing in Christ, through the operation of the Spirit, is creating a new humanity – or rather, bringing the creation described in Genesis 1-2 really and truly into being for the first time, a humanity of which the Risen Lord is both agent and paradigm. For the full expression of this magnificent Pauline vision we have to look to the great Adam-Christ contrast set up in Rom 5:12-21.

The background to Gal 3:27-28:
an early Christian baptismal hymn

We do not have formulations identical to Gal 3:27-28 in any of the passages we have been considering. But the parallels and formal symmetry to be found across them, especially the first three, suggest that in Gal 3:27-28 Paul is not making up something as he goes along. Rather, he seems to be quoting from a baptismal hymn or credal fragment well known in the early communities.[2] In the Galatians passage we probably have the statement in its original form, the other instances representing developments and allusions. Whatever be the precise original form of the statement the quotation in Gal 3:27-28 provides precious insight into early Christian self-understanding as expressed in the key initiatory ritual of baptism. As Wayne Meeks expresses it,

> . . . a resident of one of the cities of the province Asia who ventured to become a member of one of the tiny Christian cells in their early years would have heard the utopian declaration of mankind's reunification as a solemn ritual pronouncement. Reinforced by

dramatic gestures (disrobing, immersion, robing) such a declaration
would carry — within the community for which its language was
meaningful — the power to assist in shaping the symbolic universe
by which that group distinguished itself from the ordinary 'world'
of the larger society.[3]

In other words, the Christian initiate was powerfully impressed
that he or she was entering a group proclaiming the abolition of
distinctions in three highly sensitive areas of human life: the racial,
the social, the sexual. In this sense the baptismal formula has social
and political implications of a revolutionary nature.[4] If carried
through into everyday life and association it would have set the
tiny Christian communities in tension and conflict with the
established social patterns of the surrounding Greco-Roman and
Jewish world. What was the situation, for example, when slave and
master, both believers, returned from the Christian assembly where
they had both heard the public announcement that such distinctions
no longer applied? What feelings were engendered when the servile
relationships were once more resumed, as presumably they were,
at home?[5]

Not that Christianity was alone in holding such tenets. Ideas
of radical equality, including the equality of the sexes, were also
to be found in other associations that flourished in the wider Greco-
Roman culture and also stood in some tension with it. The mystery
cults that had spread from the East, with the exception of that of
Mithra, initiated women on a par with men and set aside distinctions of racial origin, class or servitude.[6] However, the expression
of such beliefs in life beyond the boundaries of the initiatory
experience appears to have been virtually non-existent.[7] Likewise,
philosophical schools affirmed in principle the equality of women
but, with the exception of the Epicurean 'Garden', hardly ever lived
up to the ideal in practice.[8] These parallels serve to show, however,
that the early Christian movement in proclaiming and ritually
enacting the overcoming of divisions as expressed in Gal 3:27-28
was not doing something totally unique or unheard-of in the cities
of the Mediterranean world. It was in fact giving expression to long-
ings for unification and equality that were pervasive throughout
that world.

As far as relations between the sexes was concerned, such long-
ings found theoretical underpinning in the widespread myth of
the 'Androgyne'.[9] According to this myth, which occurs in Jewish

as well as pagan literature, the original human person was created with both male and female characteristics. This bi-sexual origin is used to explain various aspects of relationships between the sexes and also serves to ground rituals seeking to restore symbolically the lost union. The classic expression of the myth in Plato's *Symposium* explains the sexual urge in this way: its power arises out of a desire to restore the original androgynous unity. In Jewish circles the account of creation in Gen 1:26-27 ('male and female he created them') understandably lent itself to androgynous explanation. In later texts this was pressed into service as a foundation for monogamy.

The myth exercised a peculiar fascination in circles inclined towards what became, in the 2nd and 3rd centuries, the distinct Christian heresy called 'Gnosticism'. For the Gnostics the body and the entire material creation was inherently evil and not the creation of the good God. Central to the religious quest was the attempt to escape from the limitations of material existence through esoteric knowledge and ritual. In some systems the bodily division between male and female was taken to be the fundamental symbol of the human plight. Redemption or salvation was then seen in terms of restoring the original androgynous unity and the 'myth' proclaiming this was given various forms of ritual enactment.

We can find these ideas in an early apocryphal gospel of Gnostic flavour, the Gospel of Thomas. This work, consisting largely of sayings attributed to Jesus, has as a prominent theme the task of 'making the two one', the 'two' being very frequently 'the male and the female'. In the well-known Logion 22 we read:

> When you make the two one, and make the inside like the outside and the outside as the inside and the upperside like the underside and when you make the *male* and the *female* into a *single one*, so that the male will not be male and the female [not] be female, . . . then you shall enter [the Kingdom].[10]

This appears to proclaim the total abolition of sex differences as both a condition for and symbol of arrival at full liberation and enlightenment. It is interesting to note, however, that in the Gnostic conception represented by this gospel, while male and female are to be made one, this is not so on a basis of true equality between the sexes. On the contrary, as a later Logion (114) makes clear, it is a case of assimilating the female to the male.[11] Such absorption of the female principle in the male, as found in Gnostic texts, is not without significance for our interpretation of Paul.

To what extent the ideas that flourished in 2nd and 3rd century Gnosticism were already abroad in Christian communities of Paul's own day is a matter of dispute. Certainly, there are indications in 1 Corinthians that some members of the Corinthian community had moved to some extent in that direction. We shall consider this in the following chapters. For the present we may ask whether in the primitive baptismal piece quoted in Gal 3:27-28 we have some reflection in early Christian circles of the widespread androgyne myth. More precisely, do we have here a witness to an early Christian belief that the era of salvation involved a restoration of the original androgynous unity of humankind, a belief which later Gnostic circles pushed to the more extreme form we have just seen illustrated in the Gospel of Thomas?

Certain things suggest that the myth may be not far away. As we have seen, the Jewish allusions to the myth centred on the creation accounts of Genesis 1. Although there is no explicit mention of 'creation' in Gal 3:27-28, we have noted the significance of the shift 'male *and* female' in the third pair, seemingly a conscious echo of Gen 1:27. Likewise, the parallel instances of the formula (esp. Col 3:9b-11; 2 Cor 5:18; Gal 6:15) do contain explicit references to '(a new) creation'.

Moreover, the account of Jesus' pronouncement on divorce preserved in a conflict story within the Synoptic tradition (Mt 19:1-12; Mk 10:1-12) has Jesus appeal to the original disposition of God in creation: 'But from the beginning of creation God made them male and female' as a basis for ruling out divorce.[12] This accords with a general tendency in Jewish apocalyptic thought, echoed widely in the New Testament, to see the coming or already inaugurated New Age in 'new creation' terms — the restoration or the first proper realisation of God's original intent for human beings.[13] Within this overall schema the preservation of the marriage bond, especially in its sexual aspect, is seen as the restoration of the original union between man and woman envisaged by the Creator. Jesus' exclusion of divorce is, then, an aspect of his proclamation of the Kingdom of God. The Kingdom is nothing else than a return to or, more correctly, realisation of the true pattern of creation.

It is highly likely, then, that the proclamation of the overcoming of the male-female division in the baptismal fragment of Gal 3:27-28 reflects the confidence of the earliest generations of

Christians that in their community the New Age had dawned. They had entered the world of the new creation and their relationships must reflect the pattern established by God at the start. The 'neither male and female' assertion does not mean the total abolition of sex differences in a biological sense;[14] this radical view was more likely a later, Gnostic development.[15] What the formula proclaimed concerned relationships: since status in the community depended solely upon the faith and baptism common to all, status and privileges based solely on gender had no relevance. Men and women were equal in dignity and responsibility before the Lord.[16] To what extent such equality was reflected in the roles and leadership of the early communities is another question.[17] What Gal 3:27-28 does give us, however, is a precious window through which we may inspect the ideology, if not immediately the practice, of the early period.

Before leaving the pre-Pauline level we might ask, however, whether the equality of the sexes was something that arose within early Christianity simply because impulses such as those of the androgyne myth were likely to surface within communities that saw themselves in eschatological terms. Could there not have been a more direct stimulus within the very origins of the Christian movement? Sayings and incidents from the historical life of Jesus can only be recovered to a limited degree. But more and more evidence seems to be emerging that Jesus' own personal attitude to women was marked by a revolutionary openness and freedom,[18] and that, though concealed to some extent in the later documents, women from the start played leadership roles in faith, community life and in mission.[19] If, as Gal 3:27-28 appears to attest, the early Christian community was marked by a notable acceptance of woman as equal and partner, then it appears very likely that it was only following faithfully in this respect the direction and pattern already established by its Lord.

Paul

By quoting the baptismal formula in Gal 3:27-28, Paul gives us precious insight into the aspirations towards equality in the life of the Christian communities. But what of his own thoughts on the matter? Reviewing the wider context of the formula in Galatians we saw that as far as Paul's argument goes it serves above all to assert the oneness of the baptized in Christ, so that they can come under the scope of the promise made to the 'singular seed' of Abraham. The overcoming of the 'male-female' dichotomy seemingly has little relevance to the immediate context – in contrast to the first pair, 'Jew-Greek', which so evidently has.

However, we should not dismiss the matter so lightly. Earlier in the letter, 2:11-14, Paul recalls for the benefit of the Galatians the altercation he had had with Peter at Antioch. Contrary in Paul's view to a prior agreement, Peter had withdrawn from table-fellowship with Gentile fellow-Christians. He had given way to pressure from the Judaising faction in the shape of certain brethren from the party of James. Paul sharply accused Peter of hypocrisy, of not 'walking a straight path with respect to the Gospel' (vv. 13-14). To drive home his accusation he then (vv. 15-21), rehearses for Peter's benefit what was involved when Jews such as themselves came to faith in Jesus as the Messiah. He wants the Galatians to 'overhear' the echoes of the earlier conflict because their current temptation raises what is essentially the same issue.

Paul first recalls (v. 15) the proud Jewish assertion, 'We are Jews by birth and not Gentile sinners'. But, he insists, coming to faith involved a recognition that no performance of the law availed to justification. Rather it meant recognizing that we Jews had to come before God's grace as 'sinners like the Gentiles'; that is, we had to break through what seemed to be the sure barrier between 'just Jew' and 'Gentile sinner' and accept a common bond in sin to find a common acceptance in grace.[20]

A few sentences further on (vv. 19-20), we have an even more radical expression of this recognition involved in the conversion experience: 'I through the law died to the law that I might live to God. With Christ I hang upon the cross. I live now, not I, but Christ lives in me'. The old 'I' which has 'died' through faith and baptism would seem to be the 'I' of the Jewish past which rested precisely upon the sort of boast recorded in v. 15: 'We are Jews by nature and not Gentile sinners', which bolstered its own identity and sense of significance by definition over against the 'other', seen as inferior. Coming to faith involved a real 'death' to that old 'I', a tearing down of the barrier upon which the distinction rested and a relocation of identity simply in the absorption in the person of the risen Lord, in whom all such distinctions lose meaning. Peter's lapse, in Paul's eyes, constituted a re-erection of the barrier, a going-back to the old divisiveness, in a way that struck at the heart of the gospel.[21]

We can perhaps gain a fuller appreciation of what concerned Paul here if we consider a Jewish prayer, echoing apparently more widespread sentiments, which eventually found its way into the synagogue liturgy. Three times the Jewish male thanked God:

> that he has not made me a Gentile,
> that he has not made me a woman,
> that he has not made me a boor.[22]

This prayer, which may well have been familiar to Jewish converts in the early years of Christianity, clearly has resonances with the boast cited by Paul in Gal 2:15. It asserts the confidence of Jewish male religious superiority in categories of virtually exact correspondence to those of Gal 3:28.[23] 'Putting on Christ', then, involved for the Jewish convert a 'death' to those old categories of racial, social and sexual distinction. To re-erect them, as those who were trying to impose circumcision upon the Galatians were doing, is for Paul to seek to go back into the Old Age as though Christ had not come and his saving work not happened. Faith and baptism, on the contrary, mark an entry into the New Age. The Old has passed. There has been a new creation, with the Risen Christ, the 'Last Adam', as patriarch of a new humanity. 'In' him the human race has a fresh beginning, where the categories of divisiveness no longer apply.

So it may be that the first pair of 3:28, 'Jew-Gentile', has more immediate relevance to the context of Galatians. But a wider view of the argument across chapters 2-3 suggests that the formula in its entire content has significance for what conversion to Christ means for Paul. The thrust of the argument, especially in 2:15-21, implies that the overcoming of distinctions in all three areas, including the sexual, stood at the heart of the gospel. To go back on any one would mean a withdrawal into the Old Age, the era of sin, bondage and destiny to death.[24]

The choice, then, that emerges from Galatians is very stark, the logic uncompromising. Clearly, when writing this letter, Paul takes the 'not going back' in terms of the 'neither Jew nor Greek' category very seriously indeed. He sharply accuses Peter of hypocrisy, of not walking a straight path with respect to the gospel, when his breach of table-fellowship at Antioch seems to countenance precisely such a going back.[25]

But has not Paul himself been guilty of inconsistency, perhaps of hypocrisy, in not following his principles through with equal rigour in the case of the other two categories?[26] His fighting tooth and nail for the radical equality in the church of Gentile Christians is documented all through Galatians and Romans (not to mention Acts). Yet 1 Corinthians seems to reflect a distinct temporising in the other two areas, a backtracking, even, on the radical proclamation of Gal 3:28. Do we find already in Paul a watering-down, a going back on the aspiration of radical equality in social and sexual relations which prevailed in a very early stratum of Christianity — an equality for which, ironically, in the shape of Gal 3:28, he provides the major record? Pursuing this question takes us to 1 Corinthians.

---

[1]   See B. Byrne, 'Sons of God' – 'Seed of Abraham' (Rome: Biblical Institute Press, 1979) 156-57.

[2]   See Byrne, 'Sons of God' – 'Seed of Abraham' 168; W. A. Meeks, 'The Image of the Androgyne', HR 13 (1974) 165-208, esp. 180-83; H. D. Betz, Galatians (Hermeneia; Philadelphia: Fortress, 1979) 184, 195, 199; Schüssler Fiorenza, In Memory of Her 208; B. Witherington, 'Rite and Rights for Women – Gal 3:28', NTS 27 (1981) 593-604, esp. 596-97. MacDonald, No Male and Female 14-16, 113-32, holds that Paul constructed Gal 3:26-28 on the basis of a 'saying of the Lord' current in the early communities in a baptismal setting; this saying, which Paul drastically reformulated, emphasised the putting off of the body and a return to sexual oneness in the way characteristic of 2nd and 3rd century Gnosticism. Though full of many valuable insights, MacDonald's reconstruction of the 'dominical saying' (originating not with Jesus but in Hellenistic Christian milieu), relying upon later Gnostic texts, is not to my mind convincing.

[3]   Meeks, 'Image of the Androgyne' 182.

[4]   Cf. Betz, Galatians 190.

[5]   Cf. J. C. Beker, Paul the Apostle (Edinburgh: Clark, 1980) p. 325.

[6]   Meeks, 'Image of the Androgyne' 169-170.

[7]   Ibid. 170.

[8]   Ibid. 170-73; for a comprehensive survey of recent scholarly work on the position of woman in the ancient world (including Judaism and Christianity) see R. S. Kraemer, 'Women in the Religions of the Greco-Roman World', RSR 9 (1983) 127-39 (includes full bibliography).

[9]   For what follows I am particularly indebted to Meeks, 'Image of the Androgyne' 183-89; see also Betz, Galatians 196-99.

[10] Quoted Betz, Galatians 196, n.120.

[11] Cf. Meeks, 'Image of the Androgyne' 194-95.

[12] While earlier scholars have in general been sceptical concerning the authenticity of this episode, J. A. Fitzmyer, 'The Matthean Divorce Texts and some new Palestinian evidence', TS 37 (1976) 197-226, argues very plausibly, on the basis of new evidence from Qumran, for a setting of such a 'conflict' story in the context of Jesus' own life.

[13] Cf. D. Dungan, The Sayings of Jesus in the Churches of Paul (Oxford: Blackwell, 1971) 116-19.

[14] As inferred by some scholars (e.g., Betz, Galatians 195) on the grounds that, in contrast to the first two statements, this one names the pair in the neuter.

[15] Cf. Schlüssler Fiorenza, *In Memory of Her* 211, 237; R. Scroggs, 'Paul and the Eschatological Woman' 293.

[16] Schüssler Fiorenza (*In Memory of Her* 211) puts it thus: 'As such Gal 3:23c does not assert that there are no longer men and women in Christ, but that patriarchal marriage – and sexual relationships between male and female – is no longer constitutive of the new community in Christ'. See also Witherington, 'Rite and Rights for Women' 598-600.

[17] On this see esp. Schüssler Fiorenza, *In Memory of Her* 205-18.

[18] For excellent surveys of the gospel material in this respect see F. J. Moloney, *Woman: First Among the Faithful* (Melbourne: Collins Dove, 1984) esp. pp. 8-25; Schüssler Fiorenza, *In Memory of Her* 130-54, also traces this, but insists at the same time that Jesus' action in this regard should not be played off against Judaism: his own liberating tendencies must be seen as a movement from within his parent faith; cf. esp. pp. 106-18, 141.

[19] See esp. Schüssler Fiorenza, *In Memory of Her* 160-241.

[20] I have developed this more fully in *'Sons of God'* – *'Seed of Abraham'* 143-45.

[21] Ibid. 145-47.

[22] Quoted in Schüssler Fiorenza, *In Memory of Her* p. 217.

[23] It is important, however, to note that *positive* parallels to Gal 3:28 are also attested from Jewish sources; see M. Boucher, 'Some Unexplored Parallels to 1 Cor 11,11-12 and Gal 3:28: The NT on the Role of Women', *CBQ* 31 (1969) 50-58, esp. 53-54. These cannot be dated with certainty back to the time of the rise of Christianity. They do suggest, however, that the impulse towards social and sexual equality should not simply be equated with the movement from Judaism to Christianity.

[24] Witherington, 'Rite and Rights', argues to the significance of the 'male and female' category in the sense that the Judaisers, in insisting upon circumcision as a condition of salvation necessarily relegated female believers to secondary status, since they could only attach themselves to the community of the saved through marriage. Paul is arguing for a place for woman apart from man. Witherington likewise sees (pp. 595, 601) Paul's complaint about calendar observance in Gal 4:10 as an attempt to ward off the exclusion of women from worship on the basis of periodic ritual uncleanness.

[25] Paul's remonstrance does not necessarily mean that he insisted that Jewish Christians *themselves* cease to live as Jews – e.g., by eating non-kosher meat; what he objected to in the name of the gospel was the imposition of such conditions upon Gentile converts as the price of table fellowship.

[26] Cf. Pagels, 'Paul and Women' 544-46; Beker, *Paul the Apostle* 323-24.

Chapter 2

'Not to Touch a Woman':
1 Corinthians 7

If the Galatian Christians were tempted to go back into what Paul saw as the bondage of the Old Age, the Corinthians presented him with a problem in precisely the opposite direction. The community at Corinth seems to have been a lively group, well confident that they had entered the New Age. They had heard and appropriated Paul's message that through faith and baptism they participated in Christ's conquest of the world and its powers. They rejoiced in the freedom from fear and anxiety which their knowledge of the one true God and the work of Christ had brought. Above all, through the gift of the Spirit, they believed themselves to have arrived at the full term of salvation, up and away from the concerns of the present world, which they saw to be fast passing away. Paul's task as reflected in 1 Corinthians is to confront the problems thrown up by this exaggerated sense of salvation already achieved, to 'bring them back', as it were, to the reality of where they really are at present: not totally held in the grip of the old age but neither totally removed from the conditions it imposes.

This tendency of the Corinthians to 'get ahead' of themselves in the progress to salvation showed itself in a variety of ways. They preferred a mode of preaching the gospel which turned it into a sublime wisdom rather than a proclamation of God's power working through a crucified Messiah (chapters 1-4). They vaunted their 'knowledge' and spiritual freedom at the expense of concern for the neighbour (chapter 8). They regarded the sacrament of baptism as a sure guarantee of salvation (chapter 10). They failed to see how essentially the social context entered into the celebration of the eucharist as the memorial of the one given up for the brethren (11:17-34). They disproportionately valued the more ecstatic gifts of the Spirit, seeing in them an assurance of salvation rather than an equipment for mission and the building up of the church for its present task (chapters 12-14).

15

All these tendencies centred around an inability on the part of the Corinthians to come to terms with the demands of continuing existence in the body. For them the body was simply a husk, a remnant of the old age, soon to be shuffled off. What one did with the body was morally irrelevant, since the body was destined simply for destruction. Thus the fact that a member of the community lived in a state of open immorality with his step-mother could find an easy tolerance within the community (chapter 5), while in the opposite direction some sought, as we shall see, to impose an impossible rigorism in the matter of marriage and sexual relations.

Paul's counter to this false attitude towards the body is to insist on the present dignity of bodily existence. The body of the believer, like that of the Lord, is destined not for destruction but for resurrection (1 Cor 6:12-20; 1 Cor 15:34-49). This destiny towards a bodily existence transformed by the Spirit lends to bodily existence here and now an abiding moral significance.[1] Moreover, since it is through the body that human beings, Christians not excepted, relate to one another, despising of the body and bodily responsibility leads inevitably to individualism and the formation of elitist cliques. Significantly, in the part of the letter where Paul reminds the community of the variety and mutual interdependence of gifts and services he makes the image of the body the primary instrument of teaching (chapters 12-13).

1 Corinthians 7: the basic issue

1 Corinthians is made up of a series of responses on Paul's part to problems he has heard about in the community and also to questions the Corinthians have put to him in writing. The material in 1 Corinthians 7 addresses the first series of these written questions. Paul reviews in sequence a number of issues, all centring around the area of marriage and sexual relationships: the propriety of sexual relations within marriage (vv. 1-6); whether the presently unmarried should marry (vv. 7-9); divorce in the case of marriage between Christians (vv. 10-11), in the case of marriage between a Christian and an unbeliever (vv. 12-16); advice to those contemplating marriage (vv. 25-38) and to the widowed (vv. 36-40).

In the middle of all these directives dealing with marriage and sexual relationships there suddenly appears a passage (vv. 17-24) containing far more generalized advice: 'stay in the condition in which you were when called' (v. 17a, repeated in slightly altered form in v. 20 and v. 24). The two 'conditions' Paul then cites as examples of 'callings' in which one should remain are, first of all, that of being circumcised or uncircumcised (vv. 18-19) and then that of being a slave or a free person (vv. 21-23). If for the first condition we substitute the equivalent racial designation, 'Jew or Greek', we have precisely the first two members of the triad in Gal 3:28: 'Jew/Greek; slave/free'. If we then remember that the overall context here in 1 Corinthians 7 concerns relations between the sexes (albeit subsumed under the more specific category of marriage) then the Gal 3:28 triad is in fact complete: 'male/female'.

Why does Paul at v. 17 break into the proper subject of this whole section (sexual relationships and marriage) to give this more general advice? And what are we to make of the fact that he does so in terms of the three categories of Gal 3:28? The answer to both these questions would seem to be that the baptismal statement of Gal 3:28 or something very like it was exercising an important influence at Corinth and Paul felt obliged to respond in similar terms. In fact his entire response to the Corinthians in this matter probably centred around the right interpretation of the statement and its application in the present situation.[2]

As we have seen when discussing Galatians, the formula occurring in 3:27-28 is probably an extract from an early Christian hymn or creed in common currency across a range of communities. Presumably Paul himself or his immediate associates introduced it to both the Galatians and the Corinthians as part of the original schooling of these communities in the Christian way. What seems to have happened, however, is that the Corinthians, in contrast to the Galatians, had taken the threefold statement about abolition of distinctions very much to heart. They felt that since they were already living in the New Age all traces of the old distinctions had to be blotted out.

To what extent they had carried out this aspiration in terms of the first two categories is not clear. Paul's warnings about not changing one's status with respect to circumcision and slavery may have been in the case of Corinth somewhat hypothetical. His overall point here is to counsel stability. Incorporation into Christ does not demand a change in one's outward status. The marks of circumcision do not have to be blotted out (v. 18). The Christian slave is not required to obtain social freedom (v. 21).[3] Paul's point is not to inculcate a social conservatism in the sense that the new Christian status is to have no repercussions in the present social order.[4] His point is that since God has 'called', that is, chosen, the Corinthians without any regard to their outward status (cf. esp. 1:26-31), so nothing was to be gained in his eyes by any change in their outward status; to act as if such change really would make a difference would be to challenge the adequacy of what God had already done.[5] The only important thing was to keep God's commandments (v. 19).

Whatever their situation with respect to circumcision and slavery, it was regarding the third category that the Corinthians had taken Paul's 'stability' principle to heart. Their tendency to 'get ahead' of themselves in the scheme of salvation probably meant that members of the community felt that since they were living in the New Age the 'neither male and female' had to be taken literally. Sexual distinctions and above all sexual relationships were totally inappropriate. Besides, such distinctions and such activity belonged to the sphere of the body which, as we have seen, had in their eyes no place in the new era. For a good illustration of this way of thinking we can recall the statement attributed to Jesus in Luke 20:34-36:

> The sons of this age marry and are given in marriage; but those who are accounted worthy to attain to that age and to the resurrection from the dead neither marry nor are given in marriage, for they cannot die any more, because they are equal to angels and are sons of God, being sons of the resurrection.

Considering themselves to be already partaking of this new age, the Corinthians thought of themselves as living the deathless life of angels.[6] Since those presently alive would go on living indefinitely there was no need for further procreation and hence sexual relationships could not be justified. Those who held this view would seek to impose a complete sexual asceticism on the entire community, forbidding sexual relationships within marriage, excluding the possibility of new marriages and possibly seeking to break up marriages already entered into.[7] Such a background accounts for the entire range of issues across 1 Corinthians 7.

It is easy to imagine the tensions and temptations such an ascetic imposition would create for the members of the community. The city of Corinth was a byword in the ancient world for overt sexual licence and excess. In such surroundings it would have been natural for individual Christians who found the imposed asceticism unbearable to be drawn to sexual relief outside of marriage. The temptation to seek out prostitutes and enter adulterous liaisons would be hard to resist.

So the baseline of Paul's response in chapter 7 seems to be this fear that the rigorous asceticism which the Corinthians' eschatology imposed would lead to lapses in sexual morality. In fact, it is highly likely that the immediately preceding passage (6:12-20) which deals with the total inappropriateness of relations with a prostitute for a Christian, was composed by Paul precisely to provide a foundation for the pastoral solution to be proposed in chapter 7.[8] Though at first sight negative in tone (cf., e.g., v. 18: 'Flee fornication'), Paul's ultimate advice here is 'glorify God in your body'. That is, employ your body, especially its sexual function, as an instrument to acknowledge and further the power and presence of God.

This, of course, flies in the face of the Corinthians' view of the body. But Paul's response in 1 Corinthians 7 is subtle. While he moves to temper the rigour of the Corinthians' ascetical aspirations, he clearly retains some sympathy for them. We look in vain here for a positive theology of marriage. He makes clear his own preference for celibacy — for those who have the gift. What he does is to take the Corinthians' aspirations sympathetically, go with them as far as he can, but moderate them in terms of what he sees as the reality of the Christian situation. What is most significant for our purposes is the striking mutuality of his statements about male and female rights and responsibilities. This mutuality should emerge from a brief survey of the various stages of his long discussion.

'... Not to touch a woman': sexual relationships within marriage (7:1-7)

The opening proposition, 'It is a good thing for a man not to touch a woman' (v. 1b), sounds extremely misogynist and may seem to many readers to establish a negative tone for Paul's response right from the start. Many scholars today, however, would not immediately lay it against Paul's account but see in it a slogan of the Corinthians, which Paul cites from their letter and then goes on to modify.[9] The expression, 'To touch a woman' is a standard euphemism for 'have sexual relations with a woman'.[10] The

Corinthians have concluded from their extreme understanding of Gal 3:28c that sexual relations are totally inappropriate in the New Age. This is their understanding of 'neither male and female'. The conclusion for married couples, then, is that all sexual expression in marriage must cease.

Paul's response (vv. 2-4) comes in a series of three balanced propositions stating reciprocal rights and duties between spouses. 'Because of the temptation to immorality,

1. each man should have his own wife
   and each woman her own husband (v. 2);
2. the husband should give to his wife her conjugal rights,
   and likewise the wife to her husband (v. 3).

The reason is that

3. the wife does not rule over her own body,
   but the husband does;
   likewise the husband does not rule over his own body,
   but the wife does (v. 4).

The mutuality expressed here diverges sharply from the ethos of the surrounding culture which tended to see everything solely from the point of view of male rights and convenience.[11] More significantly, however, Paul makes the decision whether to have or not to have sex stem not from what ought or ought not to be the case but from the balance of the rights of each partner.[12]

This concern for equality emerges even more clearly from the following sentences (vv. 5-6). These take up the question as to whether abstinence from sexual relationships might in some circumstances be acceptable. Paul sanctions abstinence under three conditions. The first of these is 'mutual consent', which echoes the mutuality insisted upon in the preceding verses. The remaining conditions are that the abstinence be 'for a time' only and that the grounds be leisure for prayer. The last consideration shows that for Paul sexual relations are neither inherently wrong or inappropriate in the present time — as the Corinthians seem to have held. But a higher imperative of waiting upon the Lord in prayer may suggest their temporary suspension.

Even so Paul is not quite finished with the matter but adds (v. 6): 'This I say not by way of command but as a concession'. This remark has puzzled many commentators. What is the 'concession'? And what might the 'command' have been? It seems best to see that what Paul is doing here is excluding a reason for abstinence that he regards as invalid. Pervasive in both the Greco-Roman and Jewish traditions was the idea that sexual relations somehow rendered a person unfit for religious duties. Perhaps Paul feared that the Corinthians might interpret his sanctioning abstinence in connection with prayer as an endorsement of this principle – something which would run clearly against his earlier command to 'glorify God in your body' (6:20). He hastens to assure them that there is no such obligation ('not by way of command'). Lawful sexual relations in no way inhibit coming before God in prayer. The abstinence he allows is not a matter of necessity but of convenience – something he will enlarge upon at a later stage (vv. 32-35).[13]

To this discussion of sexual relationships within marriage Paul adds a final comment from a more personal point of view (v. 7): 'I wish that all were as I myself am. But each has their own gift (*charisma*) from God – one of one kind, one of another'. Being 'as I myself am' is normally taken to mean 'be celibate, unmarried' – so that Paul is seen to be expressing here an (unfulfillable) preference that all should be unmarried. Paul, it is true, does later make clear his preference for the celibate state – carefully stating his reasons. But we should not necessarily read this in here. The immediate context suggests that it is sexual relations rather than marriage itself that is uppermost in his mind.[14] Being 'as I myself am' refers primarily to being able to live chastely and continently without the sexual expression that is a normal and legitimate part of marriage. He understands his own capacity in this regard to be a *charism*, that is, a special gift of the Spirit enabling a person to live or exercise some aspect of the New Age in the bodily conditions of the Old. But he recognizes that other Christians have gifts in other directions. However appropriate it may be in terms of the New Age, perpetual abstinence is not for them.

Should believers be married? (vv. 8-16; 25-38)

As mentioned above, it would seem that, not content with forbidding sexual relations within marriage, some Corinthians were inclined to break up existing marriages and forbid new unions. Once more, Paul admits his basic sympathy with their position: for the unmarried and the widows 'it is a good thing for them to remain as I am' (v. 8). This last phrase is normally taken to mean 'remain celibate, unmarried', as, it is generally presumed, Paul was himself. But, again, we cannot be certain that it is precisely celibacy rather than the capacity for sexual continence that he has in mind. Both the preceding statement (v. 7), if we have interpreted it correctly and what follows in v. 9, which does refer to continence, provide some grounds for the latter alternative. Whether Paul was or was not married is a question we shall take up later on. But for the present we should not see v. 8 as settling this question once and for all. What it states is Paul's clear preference that Christians remain continent if, like himself, they have that gift. Then there will be no need for them to marry.

Straightaway, however, pastoral concern leads Paul to qualify this preference. Just as he had urged married couples not to deprive each other of sexual relations in case they were tempted beyond their strength (v. 5c), so he directs that believers who do not have the gift of celibacy should marry — since 'it is better to marry than to burn', that is, expose oneself to moral and eschatological ruin (v. 9).[15] Traditionally this passing remark of Paul has been regarded as providing a highly negative rationale for marriage. But he is not here providing a total theology of marriage and we are at fault in our use of Scripture if at this point we require one from him. In the particular pastoral circumstances which he is addressing, Paul is pointing out, in a pragmatic and matter of fact way, the advantages of marriage for those who do not have alternative gifts.

a) *Divorce*

The most drastic action some Corinthians were contemplating under pressure of their eschatology was that of breaking up existing marriages. For Paul this is quite inadmissible — ruled out by a word of the Lord himself. So, in the light of this higher authority, he gives his own directive (vv. 10-11):

> a wife is not to separate from her husband — if a separation has taken place[16] let her remain unmarried or be reconciled to her husband — and a husband is not to divorce his wife.

What is interesting here is that in this Pauline version of the Lord's saying on divorce (cf. Mt 5:32; 19:9; Mk 10:11-12; Lk 16:18) there appears to be recognition that the initiative can lie with the woman equally as with the man. This mutuality of status with respect to divorce may reflect conditions in the Greco-Roman world. But it marks a divergence from Jewish practice, where the whole initiative in divorce lay with the man. We may note too that, according to the parenthesis in the ruling as recorded by Paul, the woman who has already separated from her husband is not to be forced back to him against her will: she may remain separated, only she may not remarry.

What about a marriage between a Christian and an unbeliever – a situation not envisaged in the Lord's ruling but presumably common in the Pauline churches? Here Paul feels competent to give his own ruling (vv. 12-16) and again his instinct is to preserve the union, since the unbelieving spouse is 'sanctified' through the believing partner.[17] But where there is no prospect of peace Paul does allow a separation: 'For God has called us to peace'.

In the instructions he gives to cover the various possibilities in this matter we find the same reciprocity between what is said of the man and the woman almost to the point of monotony. In both cases, whether the union is to be preserved or broken off, he speaks equally of the wife dismissing/not dismissing the husband and neither she nor the 'brother' is to be enslaved in unsatisfactory unions. As one scholar puts it, 'It looks as though Paul were labouring to express the male and female roles in almost precisely the same language'.[18] It is probably in such careful reciprocal formulations that his own understanding of the 'neither male nor female' statement of Gal 3:28 comes to light. It is not a question of the abolition of sex differences or the outlawing of sexual relations or marriage. The primary consideration has to do with human dignity: the wife has equal rights and responsibilities and equal voice in the decisions that regulate marital relations.

b) *Advice to the unmarried about marriage*

We have already discussed the more generalizing passage, 7:17-24, where Paul outlines his 'principle of stability'. This principle laid down, Paul goes on to give his own advice to those not yet married. Here his own preference for celibacy surfaces once more (vv. 25-26). But again let us note the grounds for this preference. It is not that marriage or sexual relations are evil. Paul's preference springs from his sharp eschatology, his keen sense that the present shape of the world is passing away. We find several expressions of this: 'the impending distress' (v. 26a); 'the time is foreshortened' (v. 29); 'the outward shape of the present world is passing away' (v. 31b). This expectation of 'the End' soon to come, which Paul shared with the early generation of Christians, understandably affected his attitude to the institutions of the present age, of which marriage was one. Did it make sense to embark upon a lifelong commitment, the establishing of a home and family, if only a few years more remained? Was it responsible to bring children into a world soon to pass away? A similar attitude towards marriage and childbearing might prevail in our own day amongst people foreseeing the destruction of human existence through nuclear exchange or similar global catastrophe.

Moreover, the onset of 'the End' was to be preceded, Paul believed, by a period of unparalleled turmoil and distress —. earthquakes, plagues, civil disturbance, war — a time when the faith and perseverance of believers would be put most severely to the test. Hence the many exhortations in the New Testament to 'stay awake', to wait attentively in prayer upon the coming of the Lord. Since marriage belongs to the present age — or at least involves one in duties and obligations that tie one to the present age — the married will have far more difficulty in coping with the distress of the end when it comes.

Hence Paul's advice is ultimately pragmatic. We do him no justice if we take his statements on married life here at face value, aside from the strong sense of eschatology with which they were written. When he says (v. 29) that 'those who have wives should live as though they had none' he is not trying to turn the marriage relationship into a sham. He has already laid such ideas to rest in vv. 3-5. He is simply warning — admittedly with some exaggeration — against total absorption in institutions, relationships, tasks belonging primarily to this impermanent, passing world.[19] Christian spirituality will follow him in this through every age.

Towards the end of the section (v. 32-35) the ground seems to shift a little — away from the eschatological sense in the direction of a concern to be as free as possible from worldly cares so as to be able to wait devotedly upon the Lord:

32   I want you to be free from anxiety.
     The unmarried man is anxious about the affairs of the Lord, how to please the Lord.
33   The married man is anxious about the affairs of the world, how to please his wife.
34   And he is torn between the two.
     And the unmarried woman or girl is anxious about the affairs of the Lord, how to be holy in body and spirit. But the married woman is anxious about worldly affairs, how to please her husband.

Here again we find the same care to balance equally and fully the statements about both sexes. Perhaps more significantly it is just as much the husband's role to 'please his spouse' as it is her role to please him. In fact, it is noteworthy that Paul acknowledges that marriage is about 'pleasing' the spouse. Although he ranks this among 'worldly' concerns, it at least suggests a view of marriage as a union of sensitive friendship and respectful equality.

What will of course disappoint those who look here for a more positive spirituality of marriage will be Paul's implication that pleasing the Lord and pleasing the spouse are things that go in opposite directions. There is no hint of a spirituality in which spouses might 'please the Lord' precisely in and through their intimate relationship with one another.[20] Paul's sense of all things coming swiftly to an end prevents him moving in this way towards a genuinely sacramental view of the secular institution of marriage. But again, his view is pragmatic, and he is at pains not to appear heavy-handed. Hence his final remark: 'I say this for your own benefit, not to lay a halter upon you, but to promote what seems to be appropriate and suitable for waiting upon the Lord with undivided heart' (v. 35).

Paul and Christian marriage: the verdict

In assessing Paul's statements here it is important to keep the context in mind. His theology of marriage may appear at first sight to be extremely limited. Indeed his view of relations between spouses hardly measures up to the most enlightened statements from the Greco-Roman tradition of his day.[21] But he is at least prepared to sanction and defend marriage in the context of a strong movement in Corinth to forbid it altogether. He has to reach this pastoral solution, however, without surrendering the basic sense that the all-important duty for the Christian is to 'wait upon the Lord' with undivided heart.

Though present-day Christians do not share the keen eschatological expectation that so sharpened Paul's endorsement of the unmarried state, the primary claim of God to attention and devotion remains absolute. The charism of consecrated celibacy, which gives living witness to this claim, has, then, a firm scriptural foundation in Paul. But each succeeding age has to formulate how that claim is expressed across the broad range of Christian vocations and each will have to find its own expression of the fundamental positive principle inculcated by Paul: 'Glorify God in your body' (v. 20). In the face of the Corinthian despising of all things having to do with the body, Paul insisted that it is within the framework of present bodily existence that Christian worship and obedience are to be worked out. As the most intimate living out of that bodily existence together married life surely finds its foundational theology here.[22]

Conclusion

Our study of 1 Corinthians 7 suggests that in Corinth Paul faced a situation where the view of Christian existence enshrined in Gal 3:28, combined with a sense of salvation already achieved, led to a literal interpretation of the 'neither male and female' — one that tended to exclude both sexual relationships and the institution of marriage. The Corinthians, or at least a strong group of them, were moving in the direction taken wholeheartedly by the Gnostic groups that emerged in later Christianity, the groups which, perhaps under the heavy influence of the 'androgyne' myth, claimed the total elimination of sex differences. Paul's task was to battle for a proper interpretation of the 'neither male and female' which arrests this extreme development yet at the same time preserves the genuine sense of liberation and equality that it holds out for the humanity of the New Age.

As we have seen, he defends the institution of marriage and the holiness of sexual relations. He sees the 'neither male and female' ideal realized within marriage by a complete reciprocity and mutuality in rights, responsibilities and decision-making. Again and again this comes through in the careful way in which he balances the corresponding statements. However, he is also careful to state, preserve and defend the Christian prerogative of remaining free from marriage and devoting one's entire existence to ministry (as in his own case) and waiting entirely and undividedly upon the Lord.

In the opinion of at least one scholar, E. Schüssler Fiorenza, Paul did more than strike a blow for equality and mutuality in sexual relationships within marriage. His defence and preference for the unmarried state also liberated Christian women from the bondage of patriarchal marriage.[23] The celibate ideal was not unknown in the ancient world. The Alexandrian philosopher Philo tells of an ascetic Jewish sect, the Therapeutae, who practised celibacy; there is some evidence from Qumran of similar aspiration amongst the community of the Dead Sea Scrolls. In the Greco-Roman world many of the oriental cults that flourished in the Mediterranean cities knew the practice of temporary chastity. The worship of the Great Mother involved ritual castration. In Rome there was the ancient institution of the Vestal Virgins, who were required to preserve their chastity for the thirty years of their service. But virginity of this kind was a privilege and not a right. The duty of childbearing was heavily enforced in Roman law.[24] Paul's preference for celibacy and defence of it in the light of his eschatology may have been a continuation of a Christian tradition going back to Jesus' own practice and proclamation of the Kingdom.[25] But it certainly represented a total exception and challenge to the mainstream pattern of urban culture in both the Jewish and Greco-Roman milieu. In this sense it struck a blow for the freeing of women from the automatic expectation that they should submit to marriage and the bearing of children.

Paul's problem, however, was that the Corinthians, in forbidding marriages, were going to the opposite extreme of imposing celibacy and abstinence upon all. His subtle task in 1 Corinthians 7 was, as we have seen, to maximize the freedom of all to follow the specific call which they had received from the Lord. He had to hold on to the celibate ideal, which he shared with the community, while also insisting that the ideal of Gal 3:28c could be lived out equally as well in the married state for those whose calling lay in that direction. We must now turn to his consideration of another tendency at Corinth which seems to have stemmed from an overly enthusiastic embracing of 'neither male and female'.

---

[1] See further B. J. Byrne, 'Sinning Against One's Own Body: Paul's Understanding of the Sexual Relationship in 1 Corinthians 6:18', *CBQ* 45 (1983) 608-16, esp. 611-12; idem, 'Eschatologies of Resurrection and Destruction: The Ethical Significance of Paul's Dispute with the Corinthians', *DR* 104 (1986) 288-98.

[2] Cf. Pagels, 'Paul and Women' 543-49, esp. 540-41; S. Scott Bartchy, *First Century Slavery and 1 Corinthians 7:21* (SBLDS 11; Missoula: SBL, 1974) 163-64; Schüssler Fiorenza, *In Memory of Her* 220-21.

3   The precise shape of Paul's advice to the Christian slave is obscure because of the ambiguity of the final phrase of v. 21. It is not clear whether he is saying, 'If you can obtain your freedom, take advantage of this opportunity' or 'Even if you can obtain your freedom, better to put up with (your present status)'. This question stands at the centre of S. Scott Bartchy's fine study, *First Century Slavery* (see note 2), which contains one of the best overall treatments of 1 Corinthians 7.

4   As H. Conzelmann's interpretation, *1 Corinthians* (Hermeneia; Philadelphia: Fortress, 1975) 127, seems to suggest; on this question see Beker, *Paul the Apostle* 322-27.

5   Cf. Bartchy, *First Century Slavery* 140.

6   The Corinthians' preference for speaking in tongues above all other spiritual gifts (cf. chapters 12-14) may be largely due to the fact that in some circles those speaking in tongues were held to be conversing with angels; references in Conzelmann, *1 Corinthians* 221.

7   See O. L. Yarbrough, *Not Like the Gentiles: Marriage Rules in the Letters of Paul* (SBLDS 80; Atlanta: Scholars, 1985) 119-21.

8   See Byrne, 'Sinning against One's Own Body' 615-16.

9   See, e.g., C. K. Barrett, *The First Epistle to the Corinthians* (2d ed; London: Black, 1971) 154; for older scholars see the table provided in J. C. Hurd, Jr., *The Origin of 1 Corinthians* (London: SPCK, 1965) p. 68; the discussion is brought up to date by Yarbrough, *Not Like the Gentiles* 93-94.

10   See Hurd, *Origin of 1 Corinthians* 158-63; Yarbrough, *Not Like the Gentiles* 94-95.

11   The status of woman seems to have been rising in Paul's day, but true equality was confined to small groups and had made scant inroads into society in general; see Meeks, 'Image of the Androgyne' 167-80; for survey of recent scholarship on this matter see Kraemer, 'Women in the Religions of the Greco-Roman World' 128-33.

12   Schüssler Fiorenza, *In Memory of Her* 224, somewhat plays down the significance of the mutuality expressed here by observing that the interdependence is mentioned only for the sexual relationship and not for all relationships within marriage. This seems to me to be an overly narrow view of Paul's instruction. Why may we not infer that the 'mutual consent' recommended in the delicate area of sexual relationships had an extension into wider areas of interaction?

13   The treatment of v. 6 here is largely indebted to the fine analysis given by Yarbrough, *Not Like the Gentiles* 99-100.

14   Cf. Barrett, *1 Corinthians* 158.

15   Literally: 'better to marry than to burn'. M. L. Barré, 'To marry or to burn', *CBQ* 36 (1974) 193-202, has, I think, made a good case for taking the 'burning' as a reference to eschatological punishment rather than in the more traditional understanding of 'being aflame with passion'. A more positive expression of the requirement of sexual continence is possibly to be found in 1 Thess 4:3: 'This is the will of God ... that each one of you know how to keep his own vessel in holiness and honour'. 'Vessel' (Greek *skeuos*) is usually translated 'body' (cf. RSV), but the word could also refer to the wife or even more precisely to her body; Yarbrough, *Not Like the Gentiles* 68-73 argues with much plausibility for the translation 'obtain a wife', but the following verses, stressing Christian distinction from Gentile practice, suggest that Paul has the more general sense of 'live (married life) chastely' in mind.

16   Paul seems to refer here to an already existing situation; cf. Conzelmann, *1 Corinthians* 120.

17   How precisely this 'sanctification' takes place is not explained. But there is no reason to exclude sexual relations from the overall process.

18   Meeks, 'Image of the Androgyne' 199.

19   Barrett's discussion of this section (vv. 29-31) is particularly helpful; see *1 Corinthians* p.178.

20   Schüssler Fiorenza, *In Memory of Her* 226, with some justice also takes Paul to task on the grounds that the remarks about the 'divided' life led by the married woman implicitly limited married women to the confines of the patriarchal family and disqualified married people theologically in the sense of making them appear less engaged missionaries and less dedicated Christians.

[21] This emerges clearly from Yarbrough's most helpful study, *Not Like the Gentiles* (see n. 7 above), esp. pp. 31-63. For Yarbrough the difference between Paul and the pagan authors lies not so much in the actual precepts but in the theological motivation that Paul finds in all things and his pragmatic sense of what is pastorally most advantageous for the Christian community; see the Conclusion, pp. 123-25.

[22] The final two sections of chapter 7 continue the same recommendation of remaining unmarried together with the insistence that to marry is no sin and may in certain circumstances be the right thing to do. In vv. 36-38 Paul seems to have in mind engaged men who do not know whether or not they should refrain from marriage; cf. Hurd, *Origin of 1 Corinthians* 171-76. In vv. 39-40 Paul insists that widows may re-marry, 'in the Lord', but it is 'more blessed' for them to remain as they are.

[23] *In Memory of Her* 222, 224-26.

[24] For a brief review see ibid. 224-25.

[25] See esp. F. J. Moloney, 'Matthew 19, 3-13 and Celibacy. A Form Critical and Redactional Study', *JSNT* 2 (1979) 42-60; idem, *Disciples and Prophets* (London: Darton, Longman and Todd, 1980) 105-14.

Chapter 3

Woman's Attire in the Christian Assembly:
1 Corinthians 11:2-16

Only a few years ago when teaching a course on 1 Corinthians I used to omit consideration of this passage. It appeared trivial and uninteresting – not Paul at his best. The passage may indeed not be Paul at his best, but the advent of feminist critique of the Bible has lent the passage a fresh interest and indeed notoriety. It has moved from the periphery into the centre of the burning issue we are considering.

Paul's instruction on how women are to dress in the Christian assembly gives offence. Not only does he, a male, presume to direct Christian women in a highhanded way on an apparently trivial and personal matter, but he bolsters his directive with a theological argument that seems to misconstrue the creation texts of Genesis 1-2 in a thoroughly subordinationist way. He seems to move away from and undermine the liberating and enlightened stress on mutuality and equality found in Gal 3:28 and 1 Corinthians 7. This is unforgivable. Have we in 1 Corinthians 11 the beginnings of the Pauline sell-out as far as women are concerned?

Certainly, Paul gives the impression here of being defensive, unsure, conscious that he is arguing on shaky ground. He is also at his most obscure. For all the attention given to the passage in recent years, no consensus on its overall interpretation has emerged – though on certain details there does seem to be a measure of agreement. Here I propose to set out and critically review the main lines of recent interpretation and then, with no illusion of having the final or definitive word, propose my own understanding. An important part of the proposed interpretation will be again an attempt to see the Corinthians' practice against the background of their wider religious tendencies and likewise to assess Paul's reactions in the light of his principal concerns – that is, to try to place the passage within its own context in the broadest possible sense.

Before taking up the discussion, it may help to set out the text and assess its content in a way that leaves open a good range of interpretative possibilities. This will serve as a basis for the discussion.

Proper Attire in the Christian Assembly: 1 Cor 11:2-16

Introduction: [2]I praise you for keeping me in mind in everything and holding fast to the traditions just as I handed them over to you.

First Argument (from God's disposition)

Basic Proposition: [3]But I want you to understand that the head (*kephalē*) of every man is Christ, the head (*kephalē*) of every woman is the man, and the head (*kephalē*) of Christ is God.

[4]Every man who prays or prophesies with his head (*kephalē*) covered dishonours his head (*kephalē*), [5]but any woman who prays or prophesies with her head (*kephalē*) uncovered dishonours her head (*kephalē*) — it is the same as if her head were shaven. [6]For if a woman will not be covered, then she might as well cut off her hair; but if it is disgraceful for a woman to be shorn or shaven, let her be covered.

[7]For a man ought not to cover his head (*kephalē*), since he is the image (*eikôn*) and glory (*doxa*) of God; but a woman is the glory (*doxa*) of man. [8]For man was not made from woman, but woman from man.

[9]Neither was man created for woman, but woman for man.

[10]Therefore, a woman ought to bear authority (*exousia*) on her head (*kephalē*) because of the angels.

Correction (?):

[11]Except that there is not woman apart from man or man apart from woman in the Lord. [12]For just as woman is from man, so man comes to be through woman. And all this disposition of things is from God.

Second Argument (from 'decency'):

[13]Judge for yourselves: is it proper for a woman to pray to God with her head uncovered? [14]Does not nature itself teach you that for a man to wear his hair long is degrading to him, [15]but if a woman has long hair, it is her pride (*doxa*)? For her hair is given to her as a covering (*peribolaion*).

Third Argument (from the custom of the churches):

¹⁶If anyone wishes to be argumentative on the matter, we do not have this custom, nor do the churches of God.

What do we have here? Paul begins with an introductory verse setting up a chain of 'headship' — woman, man, Christ and God; this is apparently designed to give the underpinning to the theological argument which follows. In vv. 4-6 he lays down the basic proposition, first with respect to the man (v. 4) and then with respect to the woman (vv. 5-6): a man who covers his head in prayer or prophecy shames his 'head'; a woman who does not cover her head shames her head. Verses 7-9 provide a theological grounding for this based on the creation accounts of human beings in Genesis 1 and 2. It is in them that the subordinationist tone of the passage is chiefly sounded. The statement in v. 7 rests upon an interpretation of Gen 1:26-27, which, contrary to the intention of the original, restricts creation in God's image to the man only and accords to woman the status of being simply the 'glory' of man, whereas man is the 'glory' of God. Verses 8-9 pursue this apparently secondary status of woman by recalling, in allusion to Genesis 2, that she was created for and from pre-existing man. Verse 10 draws the conclusion with respect to the woman's attire but does so in a way that contains two baffling allusions: she is to have 'authority' (*exousia*) on her head and this 'because of the angels'. There follows in vv. 11-12 a kind of 'correction' (cf. the Greek *plên*), not, it seems, to the conclusion drawn in v. 10, but to the apparent slur upon woman's status that the grounding of that conclusion in vv. 7-9 seemed to imply: men and women share a clear mutual interdependence 'in the Lord'.

Paul's second argument (vv. 13-15) abandons theological justification and appeals, first to common sense and then to what 'nature' teaches. Finally (and highhandedly) he rules out (v. 16) the Corinthian practice simply on the grounds that it is out of step with the general custom of the churches.

Recent interpretation of 1 Cor 11:3-16

1. The 'radical surgery' approach

Faced with what appears to be glaring inconsistency between the statements of equality and mutuality in Gal 3:28 and 1 Corinthians 7 on the one hand, and the subordinationist tone of 1 Cor 11:3-16 on the other, several scholars have concluded that the latter was not originally part of Paul's letter to Corinth and in fact does not stem from his pen.[1] Since it speaks of woman in tones more redolent of the Pastoral Letters they see it as a later interpolation into the genuine text of Paul. Someone dismayed at the freedom and behaviour of women in the Christian assembly sought to enlist the apostle's authority for a more restrictive policy by making this block of inferior theological reasoning stand at the head of the instructions on the Christian assembly (1 Corinthians 11-14). Thus the passage goes to join the subordinationist group of statements on women to be found in post-apostolic documents of the New Testament and Paul, so to speak, is let off the hook.

The manuscript tradition provides no basis whatsoever for this view. But it does have a certain plausibility. In the sentence immediately preceding the passage in question (11:2) Paul begins his instructions concerning the Christian assembly by writing: 'I praise you for keeping me in mind in all things and holding fast to the traditions just as I handed them over to you'. In the sentence immediately *following* the passage (11:17) he continues: 'While commending you in this I do not praise you because when you assemble together it is not for the better but for the worse'. There follows the admonition on the way the Corinthians celebrate the Eucharist. It will readily be seen that if the entire block making up 11:3-16 is cut out, there is a smooth flow of thought and expression across vv. 2 and 17, the link motif being that of 'praise': Paul praises the Corinthians for their general adherence to the traditions (v. 2), but in this one specific area (Eucharist) he has no praise for them. On a wider perspective, this 'surgery' allows for a unity of theme: there is a natural progression from the treatment of meals involving food sacrificed to idols in chapter 10, where two references to the Eucharist (10:3-4 and 10:16-17) play an important role, to the extended discussion of the Eucharist in 11:17-34. So if the statement on woman's attire is removed, the 'surgery' involved enhances rather than disrupts the unity of 1 Corinthians. The excision leaves no scars; the flow is actually improved.

For all the attractions of this view — its 'neatness' and apparent elimination from the authentic Paul of offensive subordinationist statements — it has not won acceptance from the majority of scholars. The excision of a large body of text without any warrant in the manuscript tradition is a desperate stratagem in exegetical terms, justifiable only where there is very considerable inconsistency between the suspect block and the surrounding context. Better to suspect the adequacy of our present understanding than the integrity of the text. Methodologically it is better to work with the text as given and attempt to find a more coherent interpretation within the larger pattern.[2]

2. Interpretations accepting the authenticity of 1 Cor 11:3-16

a) The 'traditional' approach – recognizing a decline from the liberality of Gal 3:28 (and possibly 1 Corinthians 7).

This view recognizes that Paul in 1 Cor 11:3-16 deploys an argument that is frankly subordinationist with respect to women. He has thus declined from the radical equality expressed in Gal 3:28 and to some extent also in 1 Corinthians 7. Experience has shown that the new freedom and equality granted to woman made for difficulties and even abuses in community life. Thus, while women may still pray and prophesy in public, they may do so only when such activity is accompanied by a symbol of their subordinate status in the order of creation – hence the directive in v. 10. Nonetheless, while basically adopting this approach, Paul gives lingering recognition to the principle of Gal 3:28 by way of the 'correction' appearing in vv. 11-12.[3]

b) The 'benign' approach – 1 Cor 11:3-16 does *not* represent a decline from Gal 3:28.

Into this category fall a number of recent interpretations, divergent in many ways, but all emerging in the end with a rather positive view of woman's role according to 1 Cor 11:3-16. Far from being a relapse into a subordinationist view, the passage, rightly interpreted, actually asserts the new-found freedom and dignity of woman. An early and influential exponent of this point of view was the British scholar Morna D. Hooker, who forcefully pointed out what had in fact long been noted: the Greek word *exousia* in v. 10 cannot refer to a (passive) authority to which the woman submits (that is, the authority of someone else [man, her husband] over her); on the contrary, the universal witness of Greek literature and usage in 1 Corinthians itself suggests that *exousia* must refer to the (active) authority, freedom or right to do something which she herself possesses. Her head is veiled, not to downgrade her status, but to conceal the glory of man, which is appropriate in a context of worship where all glory must be given to God. So 'the head-covering which symbolises the effacement of man's glory in the presence of God also serves as the sign of the new authority and dignity of the woman in the new creation'.[4]

Writing in the early 1970s the American Pauline scholar, Robin Scroggs, boldly concluded, after eliminating post-Pauline material (including 1 Cor 14:33b-36, but not 1 Cor 11:3-16), that 'Paul is *not*, therefore, the all-time male chauvinist. He is to the contrary the one clear voice in the New Testament asserting the freedom and equality of women in the eschatological community'.[5] Scroggs conceded that 1 Cor 11:3-16 'is hardly one of Paul's happier compositions. The logic is obscure at best and contradictory at worst. The word choice is peculiar; the tone, peevish'.[6] Scroggs, whose study of Paul is marked by a particular psychological interest, made the suggestion that a hidden agenda lies behind the difficulties of Paul's argument here – a fear of homosexuality.[7] Paul is determined at all costs that distinction between the sexes be preserved and shown in the Corinthian assembly. At the same time the head-covering which preserves that distinction is equally a symbol of the new freedom woman enjoys in the eschatological community. The arguments Paul adduces for the head covering in vv. 7-9 may give the impression of subordinationism but in fact they serve to point up the contrast between the old age of subordination and the new age of freedom and authority. How the head-covering is precisely a symbol of authority remains obscure for Scroggs, along with many other details in the passage.[8]

J. Murphy-O'Connor's well-received 1980 study of 1 Cor 11:2-16 marks something of a watershed in interpretation of the passage.[9] Though not the first to question the long-standing 'veil' tradition,[10] Murphy-O'Connor argued forcefully that what was upsetting Paul in the Corinthian community was the way certain members, *male and female*, were wearing their *hair*.[11] Like Scroggs, Murphy-O'Connor is convinced that fear of homosexuality was an important factor in Paul's reaction.[12] The wearing of long hair on the part of men was associated with homosexuality in Greek culture. Likewise women who wore their hair in a disordered, unbound-up way presented themselves as unfeminine and so, along with the men, contributed to a blurring of sex distinctions – a literal living-out of the Gal 3:28 ideal in the 'over-realized' way typical of the Corinthians. Paul insists, therefore, that the women are to wear their hair 'bound up' in the traditional, 'decent' fashion. When a woman exercises the authority granted her in the new creation to pray and prophesy publicly, she is to exercise this new status precisely as woman, not as 'an ambiguous being whose "unfeminine" hair-style was an affront to generally accepted conventions'.[13] For Murphy-O'Connor the arguments from creation in vv. 7-9 do not propose the inferiority of woman; Paul uses the variation in mode of creation to show that God intended men and women to be different. In the Christian assembly the difference must be preserved precisely to convey to the angelic guardians the new status and authority enjoyed by women in the new order (v. 10).[14] Thus Murphy-O'Connor draws together the chief interpretative features of those scholars, from M. D. Hooker on, who argue for a reading of 1 Cor 11:(2)3-16 as a highly positive statement about woman.[15]

In her discussion of 1 Cor 11:2-16 in *In Memory of Her* E. Schüssler Fiorenza agrees with Murphy-O'Connor that Paul was concerned with woman's unbound, long-flowing hair.[16] However, she understands the basis for Paul's concern somewhat differently. Long-flowing, dishevelled hair was a mark of the ecstatic prophetic behaviour associated with the cult of Dionysos, Cybele and other popular deities. In particular, flowing and unbound hair was a characteristic of the cult of Isis, where women and slaves were admitted on a basis of complete equality with men. Schüssler Fiorenza surmises that Christian women at Corinth, a major centre of the Isis cult, may have understood their new freedom and equality in analogy to this cult and seen unbound hair as a sign of their endowment with the Spirit and a mark of true prophetic behaviour. Paul moved to curb this pneumatic frenzy in the interests of proper order and intelligible missionary proclamation, which were for him the true signs of the Spirit. His Jewish background may also have led him to associate long, loose hair with uncleanness. Hence he commands women to bind up their hair as a sign both of their spiritual power and of control over their heads. Despite his (not very convincing) midrashic argument in vv. 7-9, Paul does not want to reinforce gender differences, but in fact (v. 11) insists upon the equality of women and men. The 'correct', bound-up hair-style is to be preserved as the symbol of woman's prophetic charismatic power and equality.[17]

Interpretations of this kind which cohere in seeing a positive view of woman's role emerging from 1 Cor 11:3-16 have not gone unchallenged. Elaine Pagels, in response to Hooker and Scroggs, asks why, if Paul were so intent upon affirming the new equality of women and men, did he select Gen 2:18-23 as his exegetical source rather than Gen 1:26.[18] Similarly, J. P. Meier finds that Paul's reading of the summary creation statement of Gen 1:26 in terms of the detailed narrative of Genesis 2 results in a derived, inferior status for woman.[19]

Admittedly both these authors work within the assumption that Paul was requiring women to be veiled[20] and it is hard to see how the wearing of a veil could in any culture be taken as a symbol of power. But difficulties remain even if 'veil' explanations are abandoned in favour of 'hair-style'. All interpretations refusing to find a subordinationist, derivative vision of woman's role emerging from vv. 7-10 must account for the fact that Paul does seem to make some kind of correction to what he has been saying at the beginning of v. 11. Why, if he has been so positive about women in the preceding verses, does he feel constrained at this point to acknowledge the mutual interdependence (or basic equality – Schüssler Fiorenza) of men and women in the Lord?[21]

Moreover, despite its widespread appeal, the interpretation of 1 Cor 11:2-16 in terms of hair-style rather than veil has not entirely won the day. In a closely-argued critique, Joël Delobel questions many aspects of Murphy-O'Connor's thesis, including the view that the Greek word(s) in the text normally translated as 'be covered' ('uncovered') be taken here in the sense of 'be bound (unbound)' and so have reference to hair-style rather than the wearing of a veil.[22] Another recent investigator of 1 Cor 11:2-16 likewise unimpressed by the 'hair-style' explanation is D. R. MacDonald.[23] I shall review the arguments put forward by such scholars shortly.

1 Cor 11:2-16: a fresh understanding

The foregoing survey has presumably shown that a fully accepted interpretation of 1 Cor 11:2-16 remains elusive. Yet progress has been made and many details cleared up. What I now propose to do is to make a survey of the passage, building on the work done in recent years and in dialogue with that work. Before moving through the text in detail, I should like to consider some more general issues – notably the question: Was it hair-style or veil?

Hair-style or veil?

Even on a most positive understanding of v. 10 (e.g., that of M. D. Hooker) it has always been hard to see how a veil could ever be a sign of authority or capacity to do something rather than an emblem of subordination and need for protection. Hence the interpretation in terms of 'hair-style' has found a ready welcome among those who wish to read Paul as positively as possible. However, it is far from clear that proponents of this view, such as J. Murphy-O'Connor, have entirely won the day.

Those who argue for an interpretation in terms of 'hair-style' rather than 'veil' rely chiefly on three features of the passage: 1. the notable absence of any explicit mention of 'veil' in the entire passage; 2. The rather odd reference to 'having something hanging down from his (the man's) head' in v. 4. 3. The clear and explicit references to hair-style (with respect to both men and women) in vv. 14-15. Let us take up each one of these in turn.

1. It is true that there is no mention of 'veil' in the passage.[24] However, the absence of such a reference is not surprising if in fact the idea of 'veil' is implicit in Paul's language. What is decisive here is the correct interpretation of the Greek expressions normally translated as 'be covered/uncovered (*katakalyptesthai/akatakalyptesthai*)'. Murphy-O'Connor argues that the Greek word(s) here mean 'cover/uncover' in the specific sense of 'bind up/unbind' and so have reference to hair-style rather than the wearing of a veil.[25] But the evidence for this is by no means sure.[26] In Greek literature the primary meaning of the word-group has reference to 'being covered/uncovered'. When the reference is specifically to the head the implied sense is that of being covered or uncovered by the wearing of a cap or veil.[27]

2. The phrase 'having something hanging down from his head (*kata kephalês echôn*)' in v. 4 is indeed a curious reference to the wearing of a veil.[28] It is not, however, so obscure if what Paul finds disgraceful for men is not the wearing of any kind of headdress when praying (after all the High Priest at Jerusalem wore a turban, as Murphy-O'Connor notes). What Paul objects to is the wearing of the sort of head attire that would *cover up* the head or at least the face. His reason for holding this is to be explained later in vv. 7-9. In any case the whole idea for men is hypothetical and only put in as a negative contrast to the situation of the woman.[29]

When Paul refers to the woman, in v. 5, he employs a common expression that would normally be taken as referring to the wearing or, as in this case, the not wearing of a veil.

3. Paul certainly refers to 'hair' in the course of his second argument (from 'reason') in vv. 14-15. Moreover, he remarks of the woman that her long hair is given her as a 'covering' or 'wrapper' (*anti peribolaiou*). These explicit references may seem to clinch the matter in favour of bound-up hair.[30] But again a closer reading shows that when Paul refers to length of hair here, he does so not because that is the issue, but because it provides an analogy which serves his argument about the veil.[31] 'Nature' in providing women with long hair and men with short hair gives an indication that a headcovering is appropriate for the former, inappropriate for the latter.[32] (We shall return to this argument later).

No compelling grounds, then, stand against the traditional interpretation that veils were the issue at Corinth. Moreover, one detail in the text argues very positively in its favour. In vv. 5b-6 Paul makes the rather curious observation that praying with head *akatakalyptos* is disgraceful for a woman because it is tantamount to being 'shaven or shorn'. It is very hard to see how having one's hair loosed and dishevelled is equivalent to being shorn — unless, setting aside all physical semblance — it is just that both are conditions associated with shame. There is, however, a genuine physical parallel between having one's hair shorn and discarding a veil. Both remove an extensive covering from the head.[33]

These considerations suggest that seeing the problem at Corinth in terms of the way people were wearing their hair raises more problems than it solves. It is neither justified nor helpful to abandon the traditional interpretation. Paul is insisting that women in Corinth be veiled when praying or prophesying. His reasons for so doing now require closer examination of the text.

a) The 'theological' argument: 11: 3-12

Here our aim must be to find an explanation which in an integrated way accounts for all the apparently disparate elements: the opening statement about a chain of headship from God-Christ-man-woman in v. 3; the parallel statements about shaming one's head in vv. 4-5; the grounding statements from the creation accounts in vv. 8-9; the perplexing conclusion concerning the woman in

v. 10; what appears to be a 'correction' in vv. 11-12. Our first attention, however, must be to *structure*.

The logical backbone to the passage appears in four sets of parallel statements, about man and woman respectively.

I. ... the head of every man is Christ
    ... the head of every woman is the man (v. 3)
        (setting aside the final phrase about God's being the
        head of Christ)
II. ... every man who prays ... dishonours his head (v. 4)
    ... every woman who prays ... dishonours her head (v. 5a)
III. ... a man ought not to cover his head ... (v. 7)
    ... therefore a woman ought to bear authority on her head
        ... (v. 10)
IV. ... there is not woman apart from man
    ... or man apart from woman in the Lord (v. 11)
    ... just as woman is from man,
    ... so man comes to be through woman (v. 12a)

The remaining material (cf. vv. 5b-6; 7bc-9) serves to ground these parallel assertions, while vv. 3c and 12b relate all to the ultimate source: God. This sequence of parallel statements suggests that Paul wants to bring out the distinctive situations of man and woman, while acknowledging and to some extent building upon the interdependence and connectedness of both within God's purpose. Keeping in mind this hint from the structure, let us examine each statement itself.

In the chain-like statement of derived headship in v. 3 one would expect that the list would either begin with the Christ-God relationship and then 'descend' or else begin with the 'woman-man' relationship and then 'ascend'. Instead Paul rather mixes things up, adding the Christ-God statement almost as an afterthought. I suspect he does so because his main concern (cf. the structural pattern noted above) is to pair off the statements about the man and the woman respectively. But Paul is also interested in locating the origin of the entire pattern in the disposition of God — hence the final 'theological' statement in v. 3c. We may note how, in inclusive fashion, a similar reference to God's disposition marks the end of the whole argument (v. 12c). But what is the meaning of 'head'?

The meaning of 'head'

The word *kephalê* evidently refers to the physical head in at least its first appearances in vv. 4 and 5 (also v. 10). But in v. 3 the meaning must be metaphorical. What metaphorical meaning could cover the three subjects: Christ, man, woman? Traditionally the meaning 'superior' has led the field and this has naturally fostered a subordinationist interpretation: man is the 'superior' of woman in the sense that he has authority 'over' her.[34] It is, however, by no means certain that 'superiority' is the major overtone. This sense does not occur in secular Greek. It has to be justified for the New Testament by recourse to the way *kephalē* occurs in the Greek Old Testament. But even here the evidence for the metaphorical use in the sense of 'superior' is slender[35] — though there do occur some isolated occurrences that could lie behind the New Testament usage.[36] A more common metaphorical meaning is 'source'[37] and this sense agrees well with the subsequent statements (v. 8; v. 12) that woman is 'from' man.[38] Thus one's *kephalē* would be that from which one derives one's entire being or one's being under some specific aspect.[39]

Drawing these various aspects together, my proposal would be that in the 'chain-like' statement in v. 3, Paul is setting up a sequence, not so much of derived existence, but of derived authority or capacity to do something. That is, by saying that God is the 'head' of Christ and Christ the 'head' of the man and man the 'head' of the woman, he does not mean precisely that in each instance the former is the ground of being of the latter (in every case this causes some theological difficulty). He means something more specific: the 'head' (God, Christ, the man) is the source from which the one immediately below in the chain derives authority.[40] Thus, while my 'head' may be the one 'above' me, the one to whom I pay honour and in this sense the one to whom I am subordinate, nonetheless it is from my 'head' as source that I derive my own authority and capacity to take action. We might think by way of illustration of someone at the middle level of management of a firm or business: such persons have the head of the whole concern as the one to whom they are responsible; but at the same time it is from this 'head' that they derive their own authority over and responsibility for those at lower levels. This would apply even to the last member in the chain of v. 3, the woman. The fact that the woman has the man as her 'head' may imply a certain measure of subordination. But that is not the main thing. The chief point is that the woman derives her own authority immediately from the man (though ultimately from God).

'Disgracing one's head': Vv. 4-9

Understanding the keynote statement in v. 3, in this way, that is, as referring to a chain of derived authority, let us now move into the body of Paul's argument. Verses 4 and 5a contain two perfectly balanced antithetical statements. A man who prays or prophesies with something hanging down from his head disgraces his head[41]; a woman who does the same *without* her head being covered likewise disgraces her head. Paul's argument rests upon a play between the literal and the metaphorical meanings of *kephalê*. In both cases the first mention must refer to the physical head, the second to the metaphorical in the sense of v. 3.[42] The man who prays in this attire shames Christ, the woman shames the man. The implication is that the honour or reputation of the 'head' is at stake in the behaviour of the one who has that person as head.

Explaining why this is so, Paul first (vv. 5b-6) takes up the case of the woman. If she is going to pray with her head uncovered, she might as well have her hair shaved and appear bald. As we noted above, the explanation for this curious equivalence seems to be provided in v. 15. 'Nature', by providing woman with long-flowing hair, indicates that a head-covering is seemly and appropriate for her. Remove the covering and she might as well be shorn. From the acknowledged shamefulness of this latter condition,[43] Paul (admittedly unconvincingly) concludes to the shamefulness of being uncovered. Thus an unveiled woman shames 'her head' and in doing so shames not merely herself but her metaphorical 'head': man. Why this is so Paul explains later on in v. 7c when he claims that woman is the 'glory' (*doxa*) of man. 'Glory' here does not mean 'reflection' but that from which one derives honour, praise, reputation.[44] The man's own status and authority is at stake in the way his 'glory' (the woman) comports herself.

With the man's attire, however, the case is different. He would disgrace his head (Christ) by covering up his physical head in such a way as to obscure the image and glory of God which he is meant to be (v. 4 and v. 7b).

In arguing the case for these two opposite conclusions regarding the man and the woman respectively, Paul is clearly understanding the first creation account, Gen 1:26-27, which spoke explicitly of 'male and female', in terms of the man only. He justifies this by recourse in v. 8 to the second creation account (Gen 2:18-25), which describes the creation of woman in a separate and derived way (woman is created from man and created for man). He is allowing the second story to swamp the balanced and equality-preserving account in the first in a way that lends a derived and subordinationist tone quite foreign to its original intent. He does not, however, describe woman as the 'image' as well as the 'glory' of man. Woman, along with man, is the image of God and thus shares the God-given authority over the universe that being image of God implies (Gen 1:26-28). But in Paul's exegesis, reading Genesis 1 in the light of Genesis 2, woman has this authority via the man. In his attempt to bring out the difference by merging the two creation accounts Paul introduces, if not precisely subordination, at least a derived status for woman.[45]

'Authority upon her head': v. 10

This brings us to the crucial v. 10. What has traditionally made this verse the most obnoxious statement of subordination in the passage has been the understanding of 'authority' (*exousia*) here in terms of a passive authority to which the woman must submit – that is the authority of the man over her. She must bear on her head a symbol (veil or whatever) of the man's authority over her.

But, as we have already seen, neither in Paul's own usage or in the whole range of Greek literature is *exousia* ever used in the passive sense of an authority to which the subject must submit.[46] The word always refers to the active exercise of authority and more specifically to the power or legal capacity of the subject to do something in his or her own right, free from external hindrance or limit.[47] In this sense *exousia* functions as a key concept in 1 Corinthians and in Paul's view of the Christian life generally as one where liberty is to flourish free from the constraints of sin, law and death. In fact a great deal of 1 Corinthians is really an extended dialogue between Paul and the community on the right use of Christian *exousia*.[48] It is clear that Paul taught the Corinthians that precisely as Christians they had entered into a situation of freedom and untrammelled access to God (cf. Rom 5:1-2). This new situation involved the exercise of those rights and responsibilities which God, according to Gen 1:26-27 (cf. Psalm 8), intended human beings to possess from the start.[49] A central right, and the one especially relevant here, was the right to come before God praying and prophesying publicly in the Christian assembly.

It is in this connection, then, that Paul employs *exousia* in v. 10, prefaced by the 'headship' chain of v. 3, which appears to ground it. He addresses the question of right attire in the Christian assembly upon the basis of the very rich idea he has of Christian authority and capacity in the universe — an authority which he sees as stemming ultimately from God mediated through Christ. With respect to the man and the woman it is not a matter of any authority which the man has *over* the woman. It is the authority and right which the woman herself enjoys — along with the man, but derived immediately through him — to pray and prophesy in public. But what about the remaining elements of v. 10? How is this right and capacity borne 'upon her head' and why is this 'on account of the angels'?

The statement in v. 10 is clearly a conclusion (the Greek begins 'therefore' [*dia touto*]) drawn from the account of the differing modes of creation given in vv. 7-9. The upshot of this reflection has been to show that the woman derives her *exousia* in a mediated way via the man. She must, then, 'have authority on her head' in the sense that her headdress has to reflect this way in which her authority comes.[50] If she were to abandon her veil and so 'shame her head', that is, the man, she would compromise the channel through which her capacity (*exousia*) to pray and prophesy flows.

In this sense the veil is not a symbol of her subjection to the man. But it does indicate her difference and the fact that she is man's 'glory' and not vice versa. Operative here are presuppositions and customs, uncongenial admittedly to modern western sensibilities, but seemingly current in the Eastern Mediterranean world in which Paul laboured.[51] By wearing the veil and so honouring her 'head', the woman stands up to pray and prophesy clad with the requisite right and authority. That authority comes via the man, but, as v. 3 has made clear, its ultimate source is God.

'Because of the angels'

Where, then, do the angels fit in? A host of explanations have been given down through the centuries for this surprising mention of angels.[52] Evidence from the Dead Sea Scrolls found at Qumran, however, has probably at last set us on the right track. It is clear from several Qumran documents that the members of the sect believed that in their prayer and worship the angels were present and, in fact, that they were participating in the heavenly liturgy

45

itself.[53] It was the presence of the angels that called for the rigorous exclusion of anything or any person involving a cultic defect. Several scholars have understood Paul's concern for seemly attire in the Christian assembly 'because of the angels' to derive from a similar idea.[54]

Paul probably did believe that angels were present when the community gathered to pray and worship. However, that he was concerned about their being offended by ritual defects is less obvious. A somewhat broader aspect of human and angelic relationships may be involved. Across Paul's writings one picks up a decided ambiguity with respect to angels.[55] They are taken as part of the scheme of things, but their activities receive no warm endorsement from Paul. In Gal 3:19 they are the mediating givers of the law, contrasted with the direct, personal and grace-laden gift of the promise to Abraham. In Rom 8:38-39 'angels' are included among the spiritual powers who will not *separate* Christians from the love of God made manifest in Christ Jesus. In short, one has the impression that Paul shared a particular Jewish view which saw the angels as none too happy about the distinctive status given by God to human beings and only too willing to act as witnesses for the prosecution and agents of divine judgment against fallen humanity.[56]

If this view of angels is operative in 1 Cor 11:2-16, then the basis of Paul's argument would be the concern that human beings, when exercising in worship their newly gained status and access to God, have clear and patent authority to do so. Paul may have thought that the angels, or at least some of them, accorded only grudging acceptance to the new status of human beings and were on the lookout for any human lapse or failing which could serve as a pretext for once again bringing the human race down to a lower level. In the context of worship, where the community mingled with the unseen presence of the angels, it was particularly important that nothing should compromise the new human status. While any kind of defect might bring this about, there probably hovers around the whole argument the sense, widespread in the Judaism of the time and found in certain strains of Christianity, that woman is where man is particularly vulnerable, especially with respect to angelic machination.[57] That is why the woman's authority must be clear: she must 'wear her authority on her head' in the sense of showing by her veil the proper source of her authority — that it comes via her immediate 'head', the man, the first link in a chain which, through the pattern of creation, goes back to God himself.

There is a sense, then, in which Paul's argument, while admittedly proceeding from an interpretation of Genesis 1-2 which implies at least a derivative, if not subordinate status for women, is nonetheless built upon a concern to preserve the dignity and status of human beings in the new order. The intent is not to put woman down, but rather to ward off any threat to that status in a context where the final judgment is still to be brought in and where angels may seek to accuse the elect before God (cf. Rom 8:31-39).

The 'correction': the equality of man and woman in the Lord: vv. 11-12

The problem is that in attempting to ward off this threat, Paul's argument has narrowly focused upon the woman. She must not do anything that would compromise human status before the angels. Undoubedly she partakes along with the man in the new status. Her public praying and prophesying attest to this. But the whole argument has been to indicate that she has her authority in a secondary and derived way. Paul evidently feels the force of the wedge he has driven between man and woman at this point and so now (vv. 11-12) introduces some kind of qualification: 'Except (*plēn*) that there is not woman apart from man, nor man apart from woman in the Lord. For just as woman is from man, so man comes to be through woman. And all this disposition of things is from God'.

Clearly this implies some measure of correction of the preceding statement in v. 10.[58] But even here the thought is not altogether clear. In what sense precisely is there not woman 'apart from (*chōris*) man' and vice versa 'in the Lord'? And if 'in the Lord' means, as it usually does in Paul, 'in the sphere of Christ', why does he ground this truth about the new situation with an assertion in v. 12 that seems to argue from what is true of all human beings simply on the basis of creation? Taken at face value, the 'not . . . apart from' phrases in v. 11 suggest the interdependence of man and woman. But why should Paul want to lay such stress upon interdependence when considering the situation 'in the Lord', that is, as Christians? It seems more likely, following a less common but clearly attested meaning of *chōris*, that beyond interdependence, he is stressing the basic equality of man and woman 'in the Lord' – an equality which the preceding argument could well have seemed to threaten.[59]

This equality occurs 'in the Lord' — a clear echo of the fundamental statement about Christian existence in Gal 3:28. However, it is an equality that goes back ultimately to the disposition of the Creator. That is why the statement of equality in v. 12a, resting upon the natural process of procreation, is bolstered by the addition that 'all this is from God' (v. 12b). Paul does not have in mind here a distinction between orders of creation and re-creation and to read such into the argument is misleading.[60] For Paul what God brings about in Christ is always the proper intent of (the first) creation, frustrated by human sin (cf. Mk 10:1-9; Mt 19:3-9), but realizable now through the prevailing power of grace.[61]

The 'theological' argument: concluding reflections

Looking back, then, across the full range of this 'theological' argument in vv. 3-12, we seem to find Paul emerging in some state of tension. In his anxiety to find a rationale for insisting that the head-covering be retained, he has reached for a traditional argument from creation. Though 'Christianised' to some degree, (v. 3) the argument hardly does justice to the original thrust of the Genesis texts. The alternative view of life 'in Christ' (an echo of Gal 3:28) restores to creation the original picture of the equality of man and woman before God. That Paul allows this view to surface, at the risk of undercutting his previous argument, is perhaps a sign of his fundamental honesty in theological terms.

We do not have, then, in vv. 3-12 an integrated, fully coherent case. We have an attempt to hold together two theological insights, to some extent in tension, but each reflecting a part of the total truth. The logic of vv. 12-13 would seem to suggest 'throw away the veil'. For pastoral reasons, which we shall shortly consider, Paul clings to the traditional argument while allowing the more radical insight to have its voice.

b) Appeals to 'reason' (vv. 13-15) and 'custom' (v. 16)

Sensing, however, that this line of argument has run aground, Paul abandons argument based on scripture and strikes out, vv. 13-15, on a new course — an appeal simply to reason ('Judge for yourselves', v. 13) and sense of what is 'proper' (*prepon*). This is not, however, simply an appeal to convention — the Corinthians could in that case have replied that *they* were following convention, or at least the convention in some Greek cities. The argument remains theological since the question concerns how it is proper to pray to *God*.

As we have already argued, Paul finds (vv. 14-15) direction about head attire by analogy from what 'nature' (*physis*) seems to prescribe concerning hair-style. By 'nature' he seems to understand the natural world as God made it, that is, before any introduction of change through human intervention;[62] since nature is God's creation it provides an indication of his will.[63] Paul clearly presupposes that short hair is 'natural' and in this sense 'God-ordained' for a man, while long hair is 'natural' and God-ordained for a woman. In the latter case he supports the contention by pointing out (v. 15b) that woman's long hair is given her (by God) 'as a covering'; 'nature' thus gives a hint that further covering — in the shape of a veil — is appropriate.[64] One could equally as well argue that woman's long hair is only custom — albeit a widespread one — and not a matter of nature at all. But Paul does not countenance such a possibility. He would presumably side with the considerable number of ancient writers who regarded long hair on a male as unnatural, a sign of effeminacy and overt homosexual practice.[65] It is probably right, along with many recent authors, to read beneath the surface of Paul's expostulations here a rejection of anything moving ever so slightly in the direction of homosexuality[66] and he may indeed be giving the Corinthians in passing a veiled warning to this effect. But, as I have argued above, how men and women wear their hair is not the central issue. What he holds to be 'natural' in hair-styles serves for him by way of analogy for what is 'reasonable' in the matter of veiling.

As if conscious that his scriptural and theological arguments have run aground and lack persuasiveness, Paul finally (v. 16) has recourse to blunt authority: 'We do not have this custom, nor do the churches of God'. It is not, however, simply a matter of authority. By allowing the women to abandon the veil the Corinthians are setting themselves apart from the remaining Christian churches. They are going their own way, deliberately being 'different' (cf. 1 Cor 4:7a) — as seems to have been their tendency in so many other ways too.

The situation at Corinth

Having worked through 1 Cor 11:2-16 in some detail, we are now in a better position to reconstruct the scenario in Corinth, to try to see what was the situation that prompted Paul's response. As I pointed out when dealing with 1 Corinthians 7, it is highly likely that the baptismal statement about the overcoming of divisions 'in Christ' embedded in Gal 3:28 also formed part of Paul's original evangelisation of Corinth (cf. Acts 18:1-18). Along with the other Pauline communities, the Corinthians heard and continued to proclaim in their on-going baptismal celebrations the good news that in Christ there is 'no longer Jew nor Greek, slave nor free, male and female'.

We do not know what steps they took with respect to the first two categories. But it would seem that their tendency to 'get ahead' of themselves in the scheme of salvation, to think they had 'already arrived' (1 Cor 4:7-13) led them to implement the 'no longer male and female' with startling literalness. We have already seen one direction this took: in the area of marriage and sexual relationships discussed in chapter 7. Now, in 1 Corinthians 11, we seem to have the fall-out of this tendency in the area of worship. As an expression of their new existence in Christ, when praying or prophesying, the Corinthian women — or at least a sizeable group of them — were discarding their veils.

While we can recognize the sense of eschatology that led them generally in this direction, pin-pointing their more precise motivation is not so easy. If, however, the veil was universally the distinctive attire of woman, as appears to have been the case,[67] setting it aside would constitute a clear move away from the conventional symbol of feminine identity, a living out of 'no longer . . . female'. That the women should take this action particularly in worship is understandable, since worship tends to actualize the salvation that, from an everyday perspective, is still a matter of hope.

If, beyond the question of identity, the veil was as well a symbol of feminine subjection, then discarding it would also be a statement of liberation.[68] In this case what the Corinthian women were about was striking a blow for emancipation.[69] And what Paul would have been doing was putting them firmly back in their place.

It is unlikely, however, that matters were so simple. We may recall that when considering Gal 3:28, we mentioned the widespread androgyne myth with which that text seems to have had some connection. We noted also the peculiar fascination the myth exercised in Gnostic circles and the particular shape it tended to take as regards the removal of the 'male-female' distinction. This was to collapse the female into the male, so that it was not so much a matter of 'no longer male and female' as 'no longer female'.

As I pointed out when discussing this question, few scholars believe that the full scale Gnosticism attested in the second century was already present in Paul's Corinth. But undoubedly the sort of tendencies that became characteristic of mature Gnosticism were already there (emphasis on liberating 'knowledge', ambivalence towards the body and bodily responsibility, excessive sacramentalism and so forth). In short, the Corinthians were already moving down this road. And it may well be that one area in which they were doing so concerned the collapse of feminine identity into the male.[70]

The abandonment of the veil, then, while to some extent a statement of liberation, would at the same time have been an abandonment of the female as well. It may have been this element, rather than the liberation, that particularly worried Paul.[71]

If this was in fact the case, then Paul was actually pleading for a retention of the female. He wanted women, when exercising the right to pray and prophesy in public that was part of Christian dignity in the New Age, to do so appearing as women and not as pseudo-men.[72] The veil was an essential part of feminine appearance. For this reason he wanted it retained.

But preserving the outward symbol may not have been the heart of Paul's concern. What disturbed him more was probably the motivation. He saw the Corinthian custom as part of the community tendency to be casual of bodily existence, to be irresponsible concerning the remainder of the Old Age that accompanied the onset of the New. Perhaps he sensed the movement in a Gnostic direction and sought desperately to nip it in the bud. The freedom and authority of human beings in the universe, being brought to fulfilment in Christ, was put at risk by deviations of this kind.

Perhaps, too, discarding the conventional symbols of male and female difference brought the Corinthian community into a dangerous assimilation to the cults and societies of the surrounding pagan world, while marking an accompanying separation from the custom of the wider Christian church. In the struggle to define and maintain Christian identity visible symbols did matter. Paul could not lightly countenance throwing them away.

Conclusion

What we have, then, in 1 Cor 11:2-16, is the use of three not very satisfactory arguments to sustain a practice pastorally and theologically necessary in Paul's eyes. The arguments he deploys to save the symbols may not impress us. In particular, we may feel that in using the creation accounts to explain the derived authority of woman he betrayed the legacy of Genesis and set in train a baleful influence on subsequent church practice and theology (notably the idea that only the masculine could truly image God). Our attempt, however, to recover the original situation of Paul, to see both argument and conclusion within the wider context, might win both sympathy and understanding for his cause.

Paul did not necessarily give less wholehearted allegiance to the 'neither male and female' than the Corinthians he sought to restrain. But his vision of what it meant in practical terms seems to have run along other lines. Where they sought to remove the physical symbol, for Paul it was social equality that mattered most (cf. vv. 11-12). We have no evidence that in this sphere he compromised one jot.

Moreover, the passage yields one fact that cannot be denied. Women did pray and prophesy in the Pauline churches. This may not have represented something as novel and removed from Jewish practice as has often been maintained.[73] What is clear, however, is Paul's acceptance of the practice and, if our interpretation is generally correct, his determination that when women exercise their right they do so as women and not as pseudomen.

Whether the women of Corinth appreciated Paul's efforts to protect their liberation we do not know. But his directive about their attire is part of a grander cause. To publicly pray and prophesy meant for Paul human participation in the liturgy of the unseen heavenly court — a key element of that 'arrival' into the fullness of human dignity and destiny that was the goal of God's saving work in Christ. Gaining and holding that privilege, in the face of threat and a scheme of salvation as yet incomplete, stood at the heart of Paul's concern. We will understand his scruple about a minor matter of dress only when we keep that wider vision clearly before our eyes.

1   For this view see esp. W. O. Walker, Jr., '1 Corinthians 11:2-16 and Paul's Views Regarding Women', *JBL* 94 (1975) 94-100; idem, 'The "Theology of Woman's Place" and the "Paulinist" Tradition', *Semeia* 28 (1983) 101-12; L. Cope, '1 Cor. 11,2-16: One Step Further', *JBL* 97 (1978) 435-36; G. W. Trompf, 'On Attitudes toward Women in Paul and Paulinist Literature', *CBQ* 42 (1980) 196-215.

2   The chief critic of W. O. Walker has been J. Murphy-O'Connor: see esp. 'The Non-Pauline Character of 1 Corinthians 11,2-16', *JBL* 95 (1976) 615-21; idem, 'Sex and Logic in 1 Corinthians 11, 2-16', *CBQ* 42 (1980) 482-500, esp. 482-83; idem, 'Interpolations in 1 Corinthians' *CBQ* 48 (1986) 81-94, esp. pp. 87-90. See also J. P. Meier, 'On the Veiling of Hermeneutics (1 Cor 11:2-16)', *CBQ* 40 (1978) 212-26; esp. 218, n.12; R. Jewett, 'The Sexual Liberation of the Apostle Paul', *JAAR* (Supplement) 47/1 (1979) 55-87, esp. p. 67; Schüssler Fiorenza, *In Memory of Her* 239, n.64;

3   For recent representation of this traditional view see, e.g., K. Stendahl, *The Bible and the Role of Women* (Philadelphia: Fortress, 1966) 29-35; Betz, *Galatians* 200; Pagels, 'Paul and Women' 543-46; J. P. Meier, 'On the Veiling of Hermeneutics', esp. 216-223; Hurd, *Origin of 1 Corinthians* 184; Conzelmann, *1 Corinthians* 181-91; J. Delobel, '1 Cor 11,2-16: Towards a Coherent Interpretation', in (A. Vanhoye, ed.) *L'Apôtre Paul* (BETL 73; Leuven: University Press, 1986) 369-98, esp. pp. 387-89; MacDonald, *No Male and Female* 65-111, esp. pp. 108-111.

4   'Authority on her Head: An Examination of 1 Cor. xi. 10', *NTS* 10 (1963-64) 410-16. A similar positive interpretation is proposed by A. Jaubert, 'Le Voile des femmes (1 Cor. xi. 2-16)', *NTS* 18 (1971-72) 419-30, who, however, sees the veil not as something obscuring the glory of man, but as something ensuring that the new-found human glory will not be compromised through any ritual or moral defilement; see esp. pp. 428-30. See also A. Feuillet, 'La dignité et la rôle de la femme d'après quelques textes pauliniens: comparaison avec l'ancien testament', *NTS* 21 (1975-76) 157-91, who, on the basis of Genesis 2, adopts a very positive approach to woman as 'glory' of man in 1 Cor 11:7; see esp. 169-72.

5   'Paul and the Eschatological Woman' (see p. xviii, n. 1 above) 302.

6   Ibid. 297.

7   Ibid. Scroggs makes the point even more strongly in his subsequent article responding to criticism of the former: 'Paul and the Eschatological Woman Revisited' (see p. xviii, n. 8) esp. p. 534.

8   In somewhat similar vein to Scroggs, W. Meeks, 'Image of the Androgyne' 202-03, holds that while Paul maintained the *functional* equality between man and woman he insisted upon the continuing validity of the *symbolic* distinctions of the old order as part of his response to the over-realized eschatology of the Corinthians; R. Jewett, 'The Sexual Liberation of the Apostle Paul' 67-68, takes a very similar position, arguing for a more sympathetic understanding of Paul's dilemma: 'One of the basic difficulties modern interpreters have with this chapter is the lingering premise that Paul is arguing for the subordination of females, when in fact he appears to be arguing against androgyny' (67).

9   'Sex and Logic' (see n. 2 above).

10 R. Jewett, 'The Sexual Liberation of the Apostle Paul' 67, cites approvingly three earlier studies rejecting the 'veil' interpretation: S. Lösch 'Christliche Frauen in Korinth (1 Kor 11, 2-16)', *TQ* 127 (1947) 216-61; J. B. Hurley, 'Did Paul Require Veils or the Silence of Women? A Consideration of 1 Cor. 11:2-16 and 1 Cor. 14:33b-36', *WTJ* 35 (1973) 190-220; E. Schüssler Fiorenza, 'Women in the Pre-Pauline and Pauline Churches', *USQR* 33 (1978) 153-66.

11 'Sex and Logic' 484-90.

12 Ibid. 485-87, 490.

13 Ibid. 498.

14 Ibid. 496-97.

15 Murphy-O'Connor's position on 1 Cor 11:2-16 receives complete endorsement from F. J. Moloney, *Woman First Among the Faithful* 31-32; cf. also A. Padgett, 'Paul on Women

in the Church: The Contradictions of Coiffure in 1 Corinthians 11.2-16', *JSNT* 20 (1984) 69-86; idem, 'Feminism in First Corinthians' 128, n.15 (though ultimately critical of Schüssler Fiorenza).

16 Pp. 227-30.

17 Cf. summary ibid. 230.

18 'Paul and Women: A Response' (see p. xviii, n. 2 above) 543-44.

19 'Veiling of Hermeneutics' (see p. 53, n. 2 above) 219-20.

20 Meier holds that the precise practice referred to by Paul is uncertain; it could be a matter of the way the hair is worn. The interpretation in terms of veils is adopted for the sake of argument; cf. ibid. 214, n. 6.

21 Cf. Meier, ibid. 221, n. 20; Delobel, '1 Cor 11,2-16' 384. Two recent studies relieve Paul of subordinationist tendencies by arguing that the portions of the text featuring such tendencies are quotations from a restrictive party in Corinth, to which Paul makes a liberating 'response': so A. Padgett, 'Paul on Women' (see n. 15 above), who finds the 'quotation' in vv. 3-7a; T. P. Shoemaker, 'Unveiling of Equality: 1 Corinthians 11:2-16', *BTB* 17 (1987) 60-63, who (on the basis of a structural analysis of the passage) sees the whole of the early part of the passage as the 'quotation' with Paul's response beginning at v. 10. In both cases, however, the transition from quotation to response is not convincingly shown. Shoemaker is also vague about where such a 'quotation' should begin; it is impossible that it could begin at v. 3 ('But I want you to understand . . .').

22 '1 Cor 11, 2-16: Towards a Coherent Interpretation' (see p. 53, n. 3 above), esp. pp. 374-76.

23 *No Male and Female* (see p. xviii, n. 1 above) 86-87.

24 The variant reading *kalymma* ('veil') in place of *exousia* in v. 10, favoured by the RSV, has weak manuscript attestation and has clearly been introduced in an attempt to explain and clarify the difficult idea of 'wearing authority'.

25 'Sex and Logic' 487-89.

26 To justify the meaning 'bind up/unbind' for these Greek words Murphy-O'Connor has recourse (cf. ibid. 488) to Lev 13:45 where the Hebrew *pr*, translated in modern versions as 'unbind', is translated in the LXX by *akatakalypton*, something the same scholar sees confirmed by Num 5:18 where the same Hebrew expression is translated by *apokalyptô*. However, as J. Delobel, '1 Cor 11,2-16' 374-76, points out, the Hebrew word can just as easily mean 'uncover' and there is nothing to show that the LXX, *pace* modern translations, did not understand it in this more common sense when it used *akatakalypton* in Lev 13:45. The LXX usage cannot show, then, that Paul's readers were familiar with the unusual meaning of the term for which Murphy-O'Connor is arguing.

27 Cf. *LSJ* 893, 47; *BAG* 28, 55, 412. Philo, *Spec Leg* 3, 60, uses precisely the same expression as Paul (*akatakalyptô tê kephalê*) with reference to the woman who undergoes the trial by ordeal in Num 5:18. *Pace* Murphy-O'Connor, 'Sex and Logic' 488, n. 28, the reference several sentences earlier (§ 56) to the priest 'removing her kerchief, that she may be judged with her head bared (*gegymnômenê tê kephalê*)' would seem to confirm that the later reference is to having her head uncovered rather than unbound. Note that in the Hebrew the priest actively unbinds *w^epara'* her head; in Philo she comes forward *akatakalyptô tê kephalê*, that is, already in this condition. It would seem that Philo (reading the Greek) understood the phrase in the sense of 'uncovered'.

28 'Sex and Logic' 483-84.

29 This is to take issue again with Murphy-O'Connor who argues ('Sex and Logic' 483) that Paul has the attire of men equally in mind in this passage. There seems, however, to be a clear build-up to a climactic statement in v. 10 (cf. *dia touto*) which states the conclusion with respect to the woman alone; this is again the case in v. 13; cf. Delobel, '1 Cor 11,2-16' 379-80.

30 Cf. Murphy-O'Connor, 'Sex and Logic' 488.

31 Cf. MacDonald, *No Male and Female* 87.

32 By employing the Greek preposition *anti* before *peribolaiou* Paul does not necessarily mean that nature gives woman long hair *in place of* a covering or wrapper − which

would indeed focus the argument upon hair. The preposition can equally as well have the softer meanings 'for', 'as', 'as the equivalent of' — which allows for the sense that woman's long hair serves as an analogy for a veil; see Conzelmann, *1 Corinthians* 181; Meier, 'Veiling of Hermeneutics' 222-23; MacDonald, *No Male and Female* 87.

33 Cf. Delobel '1 Cor 11,2-16' 376; MacDonald, *No Male and Female* 87.

34 Cf. A. Robertson & A. Plummer, *The First Epistle of St. Paul to the Corinthians* (Edinburgh: Clark, 1911) 229 ('supremacy'); E. -B. Allo, *Saint Paul: Première Épître aux Corinthiens* (2d ed.; Paris: Gabalda, 1965) 255, 257 ('chef').

35 The claim, often made, to the effect that *kephalê* occurs as a translation of the Hebrew *ro's* (lit. 'head') in the sense of 'ruler' is not well-founded; cf. Scroggs, 'Paul and the Eschatological Woman Revisited' 534-35, n.8; Murphy-O'Connor, 'Sex and Logic' 491-92.

36 E.g. Deut 28:13; Judg 10:18; Isa 7:8-9; see H. Schlier, Art. *kephalê* . . ., *TDNT* 3.675.

37 Attested in Pauline literature in Col 2:19.

38 Cf. Barrett, *1 Corinthians* 248; Scroggs, 'Paul and the Eschatological Woman Revisited' 534; Murphy-O'Connor, 'Sex and Logic' 492-93.

39 Cf. Schlier's definition of Paul's usage in this passage: '*kephalê* implies one who stands over another in the sense of being the ground of his being' (*TDNT* 3.679).

40 For a consideration of 1 Cor 11:3 that moves in this direction see W. Thüsing, *Per Christum in Deum* (2d ed.; Münster: Aschendorff, 1969) 24. But Thüsing sees the last member of the chain to be the man's authority *over* the woman, rather than, as argued here, the authority he conveys to the woman; on this see below.

41 For this literal translation of *kata kephalês echôn* see Murphy-O'Connor, 'Sex and Logic' 484 (following Allo).

42 *Pace* Murphy-O'Connor, who argues, 'Sex and Logic' 485, that the second *kephalê* in each case is equivalent simply to the reflexive pronoun 'himself'/'herself'. This makes v. 3 virtually redundant.

43 While the shaving of woman's hair may be a punishment for infidelity in modern times, evidence that this was so in the ancient world is not so easily forthcoming. That Paul, however, considered it disgraceful may be inferred from his positive statement about long hair being a woman's 'glory' in v. 15a.

44 See Feuillet, 'La dignité et le rôle de la femme' 157-91, esp. 160-62; Murphy-O'Connor, 'Sex and Logic' 495-96, n. 54.

45 Murphy-O'Connor, 'Sex and Logic' 496, does not go far enough when he claims that Paul merely wishes to express the *difference* between the sexes; cf. Delobel, '1 Cor 11,2-16' 378, 381. It is not sufficient to maintain, as Murphy-O'Connor ibid., that v. 12 excludes any suggestion of a lesser status for woman, since it can equally be argued (cf. below p. 47) that v. 12 represents something of a 'correction' to the argument deployed here.

46 See above p. 35. Often cited in connection with 1 Cor 11:10 is the contemptuous dismissal of this proposed meaning by Sir William Ramsay: '. . . — a preposterous idea which a Greek scholar would laugh at anywhere except in the New Testament . . .' (*The Cities of St. Paul* [London: Hodder & Stoughton, 1911] 203); Ramsay also draws attention to a significant parallel provided by the Greek historian Diodorus Siculus (1.47) describing the statue of the mother of an Egyptian king as 'having three authorities (*exousias*) upon her head' (pp. 203, 442, n. 47).

47 See esp. W. Foerster, *TDNT* 2.562-63, 570-71; *BAG* 277-78 (s. v.).

48 Cf. esp. the slogan 'All things are allowed (to me) (*panta [moi] exestin*)' (6:12 and 10:23). In both texts Paul quotes the slogan twice and then goes on to qualify each quotation; see also the references to *exousia* in 9:4, 10, 12; also 7:37.

49 For references illustrating Jewish understanding of Gen 1:26-27 in terms of human authority over the universe, at a time contemporary with Paul, see MacDonald, *No Male and Female* 93-94. A most attractive presentation of this truth can be found earlier in 1 Corinthians itself, in the 'chain-like' statement in 3:21-23, which forms something of a parallel to the 'head' statement in v. 3: 'For all things are yours: whether Paul or Apollos or Cephas, or the world or life or death or things present or things to come:

all belong to you and you belong to Christ and Christ belongs to God'. Behind this chain-like statement lies a key Pauline idea stemming ultimately from the Jewish tradition concerning Adam. The lordship of the universe, conferred upon humankind in Adam according to Gen 1:26-27 (cf. Ps 8:5-8) but frustrated by sin, is now held and exercised by Christ as New Adam in virtue of his obedience to God — his 'belonging' to God in this sense (cf. esp. Phil 2:8-11; 1 Cor 15:22-28). Believers enjoy this lordship, intended by God for human beings from the start, only in so far as they participate in the lordship of Christ by 'belonging' to him through faith and baptism and letting their lives be conformed to the obedient pattern of his. Thus, as Christ has his authority by belonging to God — in terms of 1 Corinthians 11 by having God as 'head' — so believers have their authority by 'belonging' to Christ, as 'head'. The same chain of derived authority is set up as in the later passage, the only difference being that in 1 Corinthians 3 the 'head' language is lacking and also Paul, remaining more faithful to Gen 1:26-27, does not separate off the man and the woman. For a sustained comparison of the two passages in 1 Corinthians see Thüsing, *Per Christum in Deum* 8-29; on Christ as 'Last Adam' and patriarch of a new humanity see R. Scroggs, *The Last Adam* (Philadelphia: Fortress, 1966) 58-112, esp. 102-12; B. J. Byrne, *Reckoning with Romans* (Wilmington: Glazier, 1986) 111-19, 224.

[50] Delobel, '1 Cor 11,2-16' 387, understands the construction *echein exousian epi* + genitive in the same way as *echein exousian peri* + genitive in the parallel provided in 7:37: 'he has control over his own desire' and takes it as indicating simply that women are to exercise control over their heads (i.e., by adopting the correct attire); earlier, Robertson and Plummer, *I Corinthians* 232. Although this sense is attested for the construction with *epi* (cf. the references cited in n. 64) the conclusion is lame and banal after the preceding argumentation and, above all, it neglects Paul's use of *exousia* in the wider context. Hooker, 'Authority on her head' 413, had already described such an interpretation as 'quaint' and added, '. . . in a context where Paul has been playing on the meaning of the word "head" . . . we may be sure that he does not mean to suggest that woman ought to exercise control over man!'

[51] Concerning the veiling of women in the ancient world we do not have a picture that is altogether clear. The evidence suggests that for Jewish women and especially married women to wear the veil in public was obligatory for decency. The Greco-Roman custom seems to have been less strict in general, but varied from city to city. On the whole, however, the veil seems to have been regarded as the distinctive attire of women. There is some inscriptional evidence that Greek women removed their veils when taking part in religious ceremonies. On the question see, J. A. Fitzmyer, 'A Feature of Qumran Angelology and the Angels of 1 Cor 11:10' in *Essays on the Semitic Background of the New Testament* (London: Chapman, 1971) 187-204, esp. pp. 187-88; Jaubert, 'Le Voile des femmes' 419-30, esp. 424-27; Hurley, 'Did Paul Require Veils?' 193-96; MacDonald, *No Male and Female* 89-91.

[52] For a useful critical survey of these see Fitzmyer, 'A Feature of Qumran Angelology' 195-98.

[53] Cf. ibid. 198-202 for a survey of the relevant material.

[54] So esp. Fitzmyer, ibid.

[55] Cf. MacDonald, *No Male and Female* 105, who cites the bald claim of an earlier scholar, Alan Richardson: 'There are no good angels in Paul'.

[56] In Wis 2:24 the fall of Adam was engineered through the *envy* of one angel (the devil); see also Adam and Eve 12-16; 2 Enoch 31:3. See Hurd, *Origin of 1 Corinthians* 184, n. 4, for discussion of this point and further references. Hurd is inclined to a pessimistic view of angels in Paul. But perhaps we should distinguish between 'bad' (i.e., fallen, evil) angels and angels who are not necessarily fallen but over zealous instruments of the divine justice and therefore not well disposed to human beings. Paul's angelology would more likely reflect the latter view.

[57] Cf. e.g., Prov 5:1-23; 22:14; 23:27-28; Sir 25:24; 1 Enoch 69:6; 2 Enoch 31:6; Apoc Moses 9:2; 10:2; 14:2; 21:2; 24:1; 32:2; Adam and Eve 18:1; 26:2; 35:2; 44:2; Philo,

Opif Mundi 156; Rabbinic: *Yebamoth* 103b; *Abodah Zarah* 22b; *Shabbath* 146a; NT: 2 Cor 11:3; 1 Tim 2:14; for further literature and discussion see Meeks, 'The Image of the Androgyne' 176-77. In making this point I do not mean to revive the old and generally discredited interpretation of v. 10 according to which Paul is concerned that woman be provided with a protection against angelic sexual seduction along the lines of that recorded in Gen 6: 2-4; for a critique of this see esp. Fitzmyer, 'Qumran Angelology' 193. MacDonald, *No Male and Female* 105, suggests that Paul may have feared that in ecstasy women were especially vulnerable to spirits and that he saw the veil in some sense as an apotropaic talisman against their attack. But in explaining the veil it seems best to emphasize authority rather than protection.

[58] The nuance of 'correction' is not absent in Paul's general use of the conjunction *plên*, though for him it is a weaker adversative than is the case with Matthew and Mark; cf. BDF §449 (p. 234); Delobel, '1 Cor 11,2-16' 384, n. 54; Jaubert, 'Le Voile des femmes' 429. Murphy-O'Connor, 'Sex and Logic' 497, admits the note of correction in *plên*, but sees the correction as referring, not to the immediately preceding v. 10 (which he interprets quite positively with respect to woman) but to the argument from creation deployed in vv. 8-9. It is surely more natural to see the correction as referring to the implications of the whole sequence, including v. 10.

[59] So, originally, J. Kürzinger, 'Frau und Mann nach 1 Kor 11,11f, *BZ* NF 22 (1978) 270-75, followed by many scholars, e.g., Murphy-O'Connor, 'Sex and Logic' 497-98; Schüssler Fiorenza, *In Memory of Her* 229-30; Delobel, '1 Cor 11,2-16' 383, 384.

[60] Such a distinction is central to many interpretations of 1 Cor 11:2-16, which tend to find a contrast between an order of creation, over which the angels stand watch, and the new eschatological order ushered in by Christ; the subordinationist arguments adduced in vv. 7-9 reflect the former, whereas in vv. 11-12 Paul points to the new dispensation 'in the Lord'; cf. Hooker, 'Authority on her head' 415; Scroggs, 'Paul and the Eschatological Woman' 301; Murphy-O'Connor, 'Sex and Logic' 493-97. The latter sees Paul's argument as 'operating on two levels: that of the new creation as well as that of the first' and adds 'this . . . gives rise to the suspicion that something accepted on the basis of the first creation may need to be modified in the light of the new creation' (494). Yet 'since God is ultimately responsible for both creations; and since he cannot contradict himself, what flows from the new creation should be seen, not as a contradiction of the first creation, but as the revelation of its true meaning' (494-95). With the latter statement I completely concur, yet still find it difficult to see how on the interpretation proposed Paul's argument is moving as consciously and as smoothly between the old creation and the new, as Murphy-O'Connor seems to want to maintain. That the angel guardians of the old order 'had to be shown that things had changed' (497), would imply at least some measure of opposition between the two orders. However, the reference to Christ in the programmatic 'chain' in v. 3 and the fact that the 'creation' allusions in v. 12 support what is said of existence 'in the Lord' in v. 11 suggests at least his implied presence in the creation arguments of vv. 7-9 (cf. 1 Cor 8:6). Paul is arguing from the *one* source, Scripture, which always speaks to him of Christ. The tension between vv. 7-9(10) and vv. 11-12 arises out of different readings of the one story of creation.

[61] A key theme of Romans: see esp. 5:12-21 and my *Reckoning with Romans* 111-18, 176-77.

[62] Cf. Barrett, *1 Corinthians* 256, who points to the use of *physis* in Rom 1:26 as a particular parallel.

[63] Cf. the whole idea of 'creation' revealing God in Rom 1:18-32; Barrett, ibid.; Meier, 'Veiling of Hermeneutics' 222-23; Conzelmann, *1 Corinthians* 190.

[64] Conzelmann, *1 Corinthians* 190; Delobel, '1 Cor 11,2-16' 373.

[65] See Murphy-O'Connor, 'Sex and Logic' 486-87, for references in this connection from Juvenal, Horace and particularly the Stoic writers Musonius Rufus and Epictetus. Amongst Paul's hellenistic Jewish contemporaries the condemnations of homosexuality to be found in Philo (*Spec. Leg.* 3:37-42) and Pseudo-Phocylides (Sentences 210-14 — text in P. W. van der Horst, *The Sentences of Pseudo-Phocylides with Introduction and*

Commentary [SVTP 4; Leiden: Brill, 1978] 100-01) include reference to the adornment of the hair.

[66] Scroggs, 'Paul and the Eschatological Woman' 297; 'Paul and the Eschatological Woman Revisited' 534; Murphy-O'Connor, 'Sex and Logic' 485-87, 490; Barrett, *1 Corinthians* 257; G. Theissen, *Psychological Aspects of Pauline Theology* (Edinburgh: Cark, 1987) 167-75.

[67] See n. 51 above.

[68] MacDonald, *No Male and Female* 89-91, gives references to ancient literature, mainly Jewish, showing the connection between the veil and the assumption of woman's inferiority and subjection. In several instances it would perhaps be more accurate to speak of the veil as connected with a sense of woman's *fragility* rather than her subjection – cf. the picture drawn by Ramsay, *Cities of St. Paul* 204-5.

[69] Cf. Meier, 'Veiling of Hermeneutics' 217.

[70] Cf. esp. Logion 114 of the Gospel of Thomas, mentioned above (p. 8). Also particularly striking in this connection is a passage from the Jewish romance, *Joseph and Asenath* (discussed in some detail by MacDonald, *No Male and Female* 96-98). Asenath, an Egyptian princess, marries the patriarch Joseph becoming in the process a convert to Judaism. At a key point in the elaborate ritual she is told by the angel Michael to remove her veil 'because today you are a pure virgin and your head is like that *of a young man*' (ibid. p. 97). MacDonald later comments (p. 98): 'I suggest these pneumatic Corinthian women in their ecstatic worship believed they too had climbed a rung on the ontological ladder and transcended sexual differentiation'.

[71] This interpretation is close to that of MacDonald – cf. esp. *No Male and Female* 91-111 – but, as explained above (p. 13, n. 2) without that scholar's distinctive reconstruction of the trajectory of the 'dominical saying'.

[72] In this sense we can endorse what J. Murphy-O'Connor has well stated about the situation within the framework of his own theory that it was hair-style rather than veils that constituted the relevant symbol: 'New status is accorded to woman, not to an ambiguous being whose "unfeminine" hair-do was an affront to generally accepted conventions.' ('Sex and Logic' 498).

[73] As, e.g., in Hooker, 'Authority on her Head' 415. Recent studies have produced some evidence suggesting that in certain Jewish circles women may have taken an active role in worship and exercised synagogue leadership; cf. Kraemer, 'Women in the Religions of the Greco-Roman World' 130-31 and especially B. Brooten's study proceeding from inscriptional evidence: *Women Leaders in Ancient Synagogues* (Chico, CA: Scholars, 1982).

Chapter 4

'Let the Women be Silent':
1 Corinthians 14:34-35

The Corinthian community, as we have seen, was one peculiarly conscious of the presence of the Spirit. In his introduction to 1 Corinthians Paul had noted (1:7) that the Corinthians 'were not lacking in any spiritual gift as they waited for the revealing' of the Lord. The presence of the Spirit was the sign of participation in the New Age – and hence something particularly valued in this community, so conscious of their new status. Yet the manifestation of the Spirit's gifts in the community assembly was another source of difficulty for the Corinthians. So on this topic too they sought guidance from Paul. His response 'concerning spiritual gifts' (12:1) takes up chapters 12-14.

The gifts of the Spirit

The idea of spiritual gift (*charisma pneumatikon*) is central to Paul's understanding of Christian community life. Through the Spirit the risen Lord continues to exert his messianic power in the church, his messianic power to subdue the universe to the glory of God (1 Cor 15:25-28; Phil 3:21b) and bring to term God's original design for human beings as spelt out in Gen 1:26-27. Each individual Christian has a share in this capacity and responsibility through the distinctive gift of the Spirit which he or she possesses. The particular gift (*charisma*) represents a concretisation in individuals of the overall power of the Risen Lord, the power to exercise some aspect of the New Age in the bodily conditions of the Old. In Paul's view, the gift is not there to confer status upon the individual or assurance of salvation. The Spirit's gifts are functional and directed to the common good. They build up the community, equipping it for ministry and mission.[1]

It is not entirely clear how the Corinthians phrased their question concerning spiritual gifts. Paul's lengthy response across chapters 12-14 culminates in the specific issue of the relative value to be placed upon the gift of tongues in comparison with the less dramatic but more communicable gift of prophecy. It is highly likely that this specific issue concerning tongues, which comes to the surface only in chapter 14, is really the main point he has been driving at all along.[2] The Corinthians, it would seem, are showing a marked preference for the more spectacular manifestations of the Spirit, especially those involving ecstasy. Perhaps they held only these to be genuinely signs of the Spirit and refused to accept the humbler, more 'service-orientated' gifts as real *charismata*.

Paul addresses the problem by asserting, first, that ecstasy in itself is simply a psychological state, neutral in itself and able to be induced by a malign as well as a good agent. The proclamation and furthering of the lordship of Jesus is the only sure criterion that a gift of the Spirit is truly present (12:1-3).[3] Secondly, Paul counters the overly narrow view of the Corinthians by arguing that a great variety of gifts proceeds from the one source (God) and all have one and the same goal: the building up of the community (vv. 4-11). The variety of gifts serves the total unity, just as in the human body the complex of limbs and organs serves the one purpose of overall health and well-being (vv. 12-26).

Paul draws this allegory of the body from his familiar idea of the Christian community constituting the body of Christ, vivified by the one Spirit. It is in this connection that he cites what is identically the baptismal formula of Gal 3:28 minus the final, 'male and female' member of the triad:

> [12] For just as the body is one and has many members, and all the members of the body, though many, are one body, so it is with the Christ:
> [13] for by one Spirit we were all baptized into one body —
> whether *Jew* or *Greek*
> *slaves* or *free* —
> and all were made to drink of the one Spirit.

Just how significant the omission is for our present concern is hard to say. But, in a context where the Corinthians are pressing the 'neither male and female' claim rather too far (cf. chapters 7 and 11), it is understandable that Paul does not wish to encourage them further in this direction by recalling the full formula once more. If this is the case, however, the omission testifies more to the Corinthians' false interpretation of the statement rather than to a retreat on Paul's part from the ideal itself — at least from what he took to be the correct understanding.

Paul's first concern, however, is to establish the variety of gifts within the one body. Towards the end of chapter 12 he does appear to rank them, placing prophets in the second place after apostles, while 'kinds of tongues' appear last of all (12:27-30). He urges the Corinthians to 'be ambitious for the higher gifts' (v. 31) and then, as if to establish a supreme criterion of evaluation, he interposes the famous homily on love making up all of chapter 13. In comparison with love all other gifts and services to the church are imperfect and temporary; without love they are empty show.

Love is, then, the supreme criterion. Having established this broader vision of spiritual gifts and laid down the key criteria, Paul is now ready, in chapter 14, to take up a more specific issue: the relationship between two precise gifts, that of speaking in tongues and that of prophecy.

A word about both gifts may be helpful at this stage. The gift of tongues is once again familiar in mainstream Christian churches. But the phenomenon in Corinth to which Paul alludes seems to have involved ecstatic, 'out of mind' states, not usual in contemporary charismatic experience; for Paul they were comparable to the frenzies of the Corinthians' pagan past (cf. 12:2). With respect to 'prophecy', again the New Testament gift differs to some degree from what might be suggested by modern usage. 'Prophecy' refers not to a foretelling of the future but to the gift of discernment. The Spirit moved the prophet to discern the application of Christian values and ideals in the new situations and opportunities accompanying the growth and expansion of the church.

While he acknowledges the value of tongues and is glad that he has this gift more than all of them (v. 18), Paul indicates his clear preference for prophecy. The criterion is that the gift of tongues builds up only the individual and is unintelligible to the rest (unless there is some interpretation of the tongues), whereas the person with the prophetic gift has something communicable to all. The intelligible word of prophecy brings about learning and encouragement amongst the faithful (v. 31); it builds up the community and, should unbelievers be present, may promote conversion in them as well (vv. 24-25).

Due order and restraint

The preferred gift is, then, the communicable gift, with the ultimate criterion being what makes for the building up of the community and its equipment for mission. But communication cannot take place where disorder and confusion reign. Hence in the final part of his response (vv. 26-40) Paul issues specific instructions as to how both those who speak in tongues and those who prophesy are to proceed: not more than two or three are to contribute, one by one and, in the case of tongues, where there is no one to interpret, then 'let them keep silent in the church'. Similarly with the prophets (vv. 29-32), as well as speaking, there is to be silence and listening and 'submission' to other prophets. 'For', concludes Paul, 'God is not a God of confusion but of peace – as in all the churches (assemblies) of the saints'.[4]

Paul introduces these regulations in a way significant for our purposes:

> When you come together, each one has a hymn, a lesson, a revelation, a tongue, or an interpretation. Let all things be done for edification (v. 26b-c).

Paul's presupposition is that each individual will have something to contribute, as a manifestation of his or her particular gift. The phrase 'each one', though masculine in form following the convention, applies to all alike. There is absolutely no suggestion that only male members of the community are envisaged.

Women to be silent

For this reason the sudden irruption of the injunction imposing silence on the women, vv. 34-35,[5] comes as something of a bolt from the blue:

> [34]Let the women keep silence in the assemblies. For they do not have leave to speak, but must be submissive, as the law says. [35]If there is something they desire to know, let them ask their husbands at home. For it is a shameful thing for a woman to speak in the assembly.

The ruling contradicts not only the clear presumption in 11:2-16 that women pray and prophesy publicly in the assembly but also the immediate context. It is not just that women are banned from asking questions. Total silence would seem to be imposed – which would rule out having 'a hymn, a lesson, a revelation' (v. 26b) . . . or a prophecy. Moreover, throughout chapter 14 Paul has formulated the regulations according to a careful pairing of tongues and prophecy. This is how he begins and in this way he will end in

vv. 39-40. The ruling concerning women's silence sharply disturbs this pattern. Whereas the threat to order originally stems from too many speaking in tongues or prophesying at one time, the inclusion of vv. 34-35 suggests that it is the women's questions that break the peace. If the ruling, comprising vv. 34-35 is excised from the text, the sequence of thought, far from being disturbed, is notably improved.

Thus the suspicion arises that the ruling about women is secondary and introduced. Paul appealed to good order and peace in the context of the exercise of spiritual gifts. A later Christian writer saw here an opportune place to insert and so gain apostolic authority for a ruling requiring the total silence of women.[6]

Certainly, the tone of the ruling reflects the sentiment and the concerns of a later period, as reflected in the post-Pauline Pastoral Letters, notably 1 Timothy, where we read (2:11-15):

> Let a woman learn in silence with all submissiveness. I permit no woman to teach or to have authority over men; she is to keep silent. For Adam was formed first, then Eve; and Adam was not deceived, but the woman was deceived and became a transgressor. Yet woman will be saved through bearing children, if she continues in faith and love and holiness, with modesty.

The 1 Corinthians ruling is not as extreme as this. In particular it avoids the (totally unfounded) scriptural 'justification' of the inferior position of woman on the grounds that Eve alone and not Adam bore responsibility for their sin. But in general it sits far more comfortably with the post-Pauline rather than the Pauline literature.

Are we entitled then, along with many recent scholars,[7] to regard this ruling about women being silent as an addition to the original letter of Paul? As mentioned in connection with 1 Cor 11:2-16, the excision of passages from an original document on the grounds of content alone, that is, without any textual warrant, is a dubious stratagem in exegetical terms. This is not precisely the case here. There is some movement in the textual tradition in that a Western group of manuscripts transposes vv. 34-35 to the very end of the chapter, after v. 40. This may not, however, be particularly significant, since one could equally argue that a scribe, sharing modern commentators' sense of the disturbance of thought provided by the ruling in its original context, sought to alleviate the problem by moving the offending sentences to the end.[8]

E. Schüssler Fiorenza considers it exegetically more sound to accept the authenticity of the passage.[9] But she argues that Paul's ruling about silence in the assembly applies only to wives, not to Christian women in general.[10] Paul in 1 Corinthians 7 has indicated his clear preference for the unmarried state. Since the unmarried woman is 'undivided' in her waiting upon the Lord, since her concern is entirely how 'she may be holy in body and spirit', it may be presumed that Paul would allow her full participation in the assembly, while insisting that married women must hold their questions till they can ask their husbands at home.

But to defend the authenticity of Paul's ruling by seeing it restricted to married women only is not convincing. Paul would hardly forbid a mature married woman from public prophecy and prayer, while granting the privilege to her young unmarried daughter simply on the basis that the latter was not married.[11] Moreover, married couples participated prominently in Christian life and mission.[12] Are we to imagine Paul's married friend and co-missionary, Prisca, the instructress of Apollos according to Acts 18:26, sitting reduced to silence while younger, unmarried women spoke up? It seems, then, that the attempt to resolve the discrepancy between 1 Cor 14:34-35 and the wider Pauline context by interpreting the ruling in terms of wives only raises more difficulties than it solves. The passage is glaringly inconsistent with Paul's statements elsewhere. Is it sufficiently so to warrant the conclusion that it is not authentically Pauline?

My sense is that this is a reasonable exegetical judgment to make. The wording of vv. 34-35 has much affinity to that of the immediately preceding context. But this does not mean that it was once part of that context. Rather, a later church official, concerned as was Paul for order and peace in the assembly, but seeing the threat to order coming from the participation of women, took Paul's language about being 'silent in the assembly' (v. 28) and being 'submissive' (v. 32) and constructed from this the ruling about women now appearing in the text.

That there was ample opportunity for such insertions to take place cannot be denied. The collection and wider publication of Paul's letters was precisely the achievement of the post-Pauline school to which presumably the author of the ruling belonged. We have only to look as far as 2 Corinthians to find evidence of compilation and insertion on a far more complex scale.[13]

Conclusion

Paul was not then responsible for enjoining silence upon women in church, any more than he was responsible for the even more offensive form of this injunction appearing amongst the Pastoral Letters. Such a ruling did, however, go out under his name and forms a potent element of the Pauline myth in the consciousness of many Christians, notably women. The historical damage done through such attribution cannot be undone. Our investigation, however, has shown how Paul valued the spiritual gift of each and every Christian — an impulse, surely, to greater, more inclusive participation in sharing spiritual gifts today.

---

[1] For this view of *charisma* in Paul see the classic essay of E. Käsemann, 'Ministry and Community in the New Testament' in *Essays on New Testament Themes* (London: SCM, 1964) 63-94, esp. pp. 63-75.

[2] Cf. Hurd, *Origin of 1 Corinthians* 186-95, esp. p. 192.

[3] Cf. Conzelmann, *1 Corinthians* 206.

[4] That is, reading v. 33 as a unit, rather than attaching the final phrase to the following injunction concerning women; on this see Barrett, *1 Corinthians* 329-30; also J. Murphy-O'Connor, 'Interpolations in 1 Corinthians' 90.

[5] If, as I shall argue, this injunction is taken to be an interpolation into the original text, the rhetorical question, making up v. 36, is best seen as the original ending to the whole paragraph, following v. 33a; the 'word of God' refers explicitly to the gift of prophecy; see Barrett *1 Corinthians* 330. This effectively excludes D. W. Odell-Scott's attempt to argue for an overall positive interpretation of the passage (vv. 33b-36) on the basis that v. 36 represents a rhetorical rebuttal on Paul's part of a chauvinistic ruling emanating from male members of the community cited in vv. 33b-35: 'Let the Women Speak in the Church. An Egalitarian Interpretation of 1 Cor 14:33b-36', *BTB* 13 (1983) 90-93.

[6] A further consideration supporting this conclusion would be the appeal to what 'the law says' (v. 34) — something quite uncharacteristic of Paul, as is also the use of the verb *epitrepesthai* in the same verse.

[7] E.g., Barrett, *1 Corinthians* 330-333 (preferred though certain); Conzelmann, *1 Corinthians* 246; Jewett, 'Sexual Liberation of the Apostle Paul' 59; Scroggs, 'Paul and the Eschatological Woman' 284; idem. 'Paul and the Eschatological Woman Revisited' 533; Pagels, 'Paul and Women' 544; Murphy-O'Connor, 'Interpolations in 1 Corinthians' 90-92'. For a thorough review of the question see Feuillet, 'La dignité de le rôle de la femme' 162-70 (arguing for authenticity).

[8] Cf. Barrett, *1 Corinthians* 330.

[9] *In Memory of Her* 230.

[10] Ibid. 231.

[11] Cf. Murphy-O'Connor, 'Interpolations in 1 Corinthians' 91.

[12] In view of this Professor Schüssler Fiorenza herself finds the ruling 'surprising'.

[13] Notably the highly intrusive passage comprising 2 Cor 6:14 - 7:1. But the entire sequence of the letter is problematic, suggesting to many scholars that it represents a compilation of several letters rather than a single document. On the more general issue of criteria for recognizing interpolations in the Pauline letters see W. O. Walker, Jr., 'The Burden of Proof in Identifying Interpolations in the Pauline Letters', *NTS* 33 (1987) 610-618.

Chapter 5

Women as Paul's Co-Workers

So far we have been examining the fairly obvious passages in Paul's writings that shed light on his attitude to women. Recent studies, however, have unearthed much information about the role of women in the Pauline communities from far less likely places. From remarks and comments Paul makes, especially when sending greetings, scholars have built up an impressive picture showing the vigorous involvement of women in Christian life and mission. Without a consideration of the apparently large-scale collaboration of women in Paul's life and ministry the survey drawn simply from the more explicit passages would be unbalanced and incomplete.

Our view of church life in the early period has been built up very much from the Acts of the Apostles. Acts does indeed testify to the importance of women in Paul's ministry. The most obvious example of this is Lydia of Thyatira, who heard Paul speak at Philippi and became his first convert in Europe (16:14-15). Besides offering Paul hospitality, it would seem that her house became the centre of the nascent Christian community in Philippi (v. 40). Lydia is probably a typical and early example of a constant pattern whereby wealthy and prominent women act as patrons and protectors of the early Christian movement.[1]

While it undoubedly contains much information about the early decades, Acts stems from a relatively late period in the New Testament era, close to the time of the Pastoral Letters. Its picture of the Pauline churches is undoubtedly coloured by the church structures and concerns of its own time. So there is good reason to suspect that if women played a more active role in church ministry in the early period, this would not necessarily be represented in Acts and may in fact have been suppressed under the kind of androcentric pressure reflected in the Pastorals. Thus the picture in Acts, where prominent and wealthy women function as local supporters of Paul, has to be filled out through a socio-historical examination of the authentically Pauline material.[2] From this a much more dynamic involvement of women emerges.

It would appear that the institutional set-up of early Christianity fell into two patterns: the more or less stable local communities organized around a cluster of households and the itinerant missionary agents who moved from community to community. The latter served as a bond of unity between the local communities and in return received hospitality and support. They were a principal means of spreading the gospel (though Christians travelling on business and trade across the excellent roads of the Empire were also key agents in this process). It must be remembered that it was Paul's practice to exercise his trade when on his missionary journeys (cf. 1 Cor 9:15-18; 2 Cor 11:9; 12:13; 1 Thess 2:9). The prime purpose of this may have been, as he claimed, to relieve the local communities of financial burden. But undoubtedly finding employment among fellow tradespeople afforded much opportunity for quiet person-to-person sharing of the faith and this, rather than formal preaching, may have been the principal means of its extension. In any case, the ministry of Paul and his immediate co-workers (such as Timothy, Titus, Tychicus) clearly falls into this category of itinerant missionary.[3]

Whereas the Lucan picture, as we have noted, would seem to confine the role of women chiefly to that of support and patronage on the local scene, there are clues in the Pauline letters that they also had a share in his more mobile missionary work. Let us examine some of the material.

Evodia and Syntyche

Writing to the Philippians Paul makes an appeal for reconciliation between two prominent female members of the community (4:2-3):

> I entreat Evodia and I entreat Syntyche to agree in the Lord. And I ask you, true yokefellow, help these women, for they have laboured side by side with me in the gospel together with Clement and the rest of my fellow workers, whose names are written in the book of life.

We do not know the identity of the 'true yokefellow' whom Paul requests to help in the reconciliation (the Greek noun may represent in fact a proper name, 'Syzygus').[4] What is clear, however, is that Evodia and Syntyche were members of such prominence and significance that their estrangement posed a serious hindrance to community life. It may be that their households provided the nucleus of two house churches within the wider Philippian community, in which case their quarrel would have threatened the entire body with schism. On the other hand, Paul's subsequent tribute to both in the appeal to the 'yokefellow' suggests a wider role. If they have 'struggled side by side with me' (*synathlêtein* – as of athletes contending in the arena) in the work of the gospel, if they are ranked along with Clement and all his fellow-workers (*synergoi*), then their ministry would seem to have taken a similar shape: they have engaged alongside Paul and his apostolic band in the missionary propagation of the gospel.[5] As such they may have acted as representatives of the Philippian community, which seems to have entered into a formal partnership with Paul in sharing his missionary work (cf. Phil 1:5; 4:15).[6]

The greetings in Romans 16

The concluding chapter of the Letter to the Romans contains a long series of greetings many of which throw much light upon the ministry of women in the Pauline churches. It is worth citing the relevant material:

[1]I commend to you our sister *Phoebe*, a deacon (*diakonos*) of the church at Cenchrae, [2]that you may receive her in the Lord as befits the saints, and help her in whatever she may require from you, for she has been a helper (*prostatis*) of many and of myself as well.

[3]Greet *Prisca and Aquila*, my fellow workers in Christ Jesus, [4]who risked their necks for my life, to whom not only I but also all the churches of the Gentiles give thanks; [5]greet also the church in their house. ... [6]Greet *Mary*, who has worked hard among you.

[7]Greet Andronicus and *Junias*, my relatives and my fellow prisoners; they are persons of repute among the apostles, and they were in Christ before me.

[12]Greet those workers in the Lord, *Tryphaena* and *Tryphosa*. Greet the beloved Persis, who has worked hard in the Lord.

a) Phoebe

Phoebe (v. 1) is normally referred to in the standard translations (cf. RSV; Jerusalem Bible) as 'deaconess' and her role is then understood in terms of that played by deaconesses in the later church, that is, non-ordained feminine church workers, chiefly involved in instruction of the young and charitable relief. But this is misleading and anachronistic. Paul uses of Phoebe the word *diakonos*, which he regularly employs to describe his own ministry of the word (cf. especially 1 Cor 3:5; 2 Cor 3:1-11). It characterizes the one who hands out or facilitates the distribution of some benefit or service — from the simple waiter at a table to an officer commissioned by a superior for some particular task. If Phoebe is commended to the Roman Christians as a 'deacon of the church at Cenchrae (virtually a twin city of Corinth)', it is quite likely that she is not simply a helper or patroness in the local community, but a teacher and possibly a missionary of that church.[7] The subsequent reference to her as *prostatis* 'of many and of myself as well' suggests not merely help in a general kind of way. *Prostatis* is used in contemporary literature of the patronage given by goddesses and women of high station.[8] Clearly Phoebe is a Christian of considerable stature, one who shares responsibility for mission with Paul, possibly at times in an itinerant way, as Paul's commendation of her to the Roman community suggests.

b) Prisca and Aquila

Prisca (or Priscilla) and Aquila were a married couple, friends of Paul. The comparatively frequent references to them in Acts and the letters testify to their effective and widespread ministry in the Pauline period. Aquila, originally a native of Pontus, on the Black Sea, seems to have been in the first place a Jewish Christian of the Roman community. According to Acts 18:1-3, he with his wife, having been expelled from Rome along with all Jews under the Emperor Claudius, met Paul in Corinth on the latter's first arrival there. Apart from the faith, they shared with Paul a common trade, tentmaking, which doubtless forged an even closer bond. They left Corinth with Paul and came to Ephesus, where they stayed while he returned to Caesarea and Antioch in Syria (Acts 18:18-21). During this period they undertook the fuller instruction of the formidable Apollos (v. 26), later to become Paul's co-worker:

[24]Now a Jew named Apollos, a native of Alexandria, came to Ephesus. He was an eloquent man, well versed in the scriptures. [25]He had been instructed in the way of the Lord; and being fervent in spirit, he spoke and taught accurately the things concerning Jesus, though he knew only the baptism of John. [26]He began to speak boldly in the synagogue; but when Priscilla and Aquila heard him, they took him and expounded to him the way of God more accurately.

Significantly, perhaps, in the reference to the instruction of this 'eloquent man, well-versed in the Scriptures', it is Prisca's name that is mentioned first, suggesting that she may have taken the major part.[9]

Writing later from Ephesus to the church at Corinth, Paul in 1 Corinthians (16:19) sends 'hearty greetings in the Lord' from 'Aquila and Prisca, together with the church in their house'. At this point the couple are still in Ephesus. By the time Paul writes the letter to the Romans during his third and final stay in Corinth, the couple have returned to Rome where again there is a 'church in their house'. In the greeting cited above (Rom 16:3-5) Paul speaks of them as his 'fellow workers' (*synergoi*). They have 'risked their necks' for his life and are owed a debt of gratitude by all the Gentile churches. Such language can only mean that this married couple worked alongside Paul in the ministry of the word. The fact that house churches seem to have been established in their household in at least two cities where they stayed may suggest that their ministry involved longer stays in particular places. Nonetheless, it is also clear that they shared something of Paul's more mobile mission and left their influence throughout the Gentile churches. In short, they testify to the vigorous and effective involvement of a married couple in the Christian mission – with some indication that it was the wife, Prisca, who took the leading role.

Paul himself, of course, as we have seen, made clear in 1 Corinthians 7 his own preference for the unmarried state as providing better opportunity for 'waiting upon the Lord with undivided heart' (v. 35). What Prisca's reaction to this statement might have been, if Paul showed or discussed with her a draft of the letter he was preparing for Corinth, we can only conjecture. His own missionary practice was to go about with male associates rather than a '(Christian) sister, as wife', as was the acknowledged right and custom of other apostles (1 Cor 9:4).[10] Though he met criticism on this score (cf. 2 Cor 11:7-11; 12:13), his reason for fore-going the privilege was not misogynist, but economic and pastoral. He and his companions sought always to toil with their own hands – earn their upkeep, so as not to burden the host churches. It may well have been that in the prevailing social circumstances, a 'sister' companion would not easily have found opportunity to find work and so share in this practice. However, the fact that his own practice was regarded as exceptional may further serve to indicate the extent to which married women participated in the itinerant mission in the early decades.

c) Andronicus and Junia(s)

Alongside Prisca and Aquila in Paul's greetings we have Andronicus and Junia(s). In the short appendage to the greeting (v. 7) Paul gives us quite a bit of information about this pair. They were related to him, they had been converted to Christianity (lit. 'were in Christ') before him and, most interestingly, they are 'persons of repute among the apostles'. The question is whether the second name 'Junia(s)' designates a woman. Until recently most scholars simply took it as unthinkable that the title 'apostle' could in any way apply to a woman. The word occurring here, *Iounian*, was understood as the accusative of a masculine form, *Iounias*. Such an understanding, however, has to fly in the face of the fact that *Iounias* is not attested as a masculine name; what occurs here in Paul's greeting has to be understood as an abbreviation, not otherwise found, of the longer, *Iounianos*, a Greek form of the Latin name *Iunianus*. It is far more reasonable to put aside prejudices about whether women could or could not be apostles and to assume that what we have here is the accusative of the feminine name, *Iounia*, which in its Latin form, Junia, is attested as a woman's name in the Hellenistic world of the Roman empire. Certainly, several early Church fathers understood it this way — notably Chrysostom, who, far from having difficulties with the fact that a woman bears the title 'apostle', actually exclaims in wonder and praise at the devotion of this woman that she should be counted worthy of the name.[11] If we should, then, along with many recent scholars,[12] rejoin this ancient opinion that the reference here is to a woman, then not merely do we have another married couple, Andronicus and Junia, employed in the Christian mission but we have a woman listed as an apostle — and an outstanding apostle at that.

'Apostle' here should not, of course, be understood in the popular sense of the twelve original companions of Jesus. This is a Lucan retrojection of the title back into the time of Jesus' historical ministry. 'Apostle' in the Pauline sense, which also occurs in Acts, designated a privileged group who had both 'seen the Lord' (that is, had been witnesses to the resurrection) and had been commissioned by him to preach and found churches. It denotes the foundational and leading (cf. 1 Cor 12:28) rank of those responsible for the Christian mission. Considering the high esteem Paul has for this role and his vigorous defence of his own sharing in it, the tribute paid to Andronicus and Junia is very high indeed and one of very considerable significance for the engagement of women in the early Christian mission.

d) Mary, Tryphaena and Tryphosa

Finally, among those greeted in Romans 16 we find women such as Mary 'who has worked hard among you' (v. 6) and Tryphaena and Tryphosa, 'those workers in the Lord' (v. 12). The term Paul uses to refer to the 'working' of these women, *kopian*, is precisely the same verb he employs to describe his own apostolic labours (cf. e.g., 1 Cor 15:10). Again, we find Paul acknowledging the role of Christian women in apostolic labours similar to his own.

Conclusion

From these simple greetings a picture emerges which may only be the tip of an iceberg as far as the full extent of women's ministry in the early period goes. Paul undoubedly did not initiate such ministry. He presumably found it in operation, worked with it and apparently regarded it as normal. More than this, the language of the greetings suggests great warmth, appreciation and even intimacy in the relationships with such female collaborators. If later generations saw fit to curtail and even forbid the engagement of women in the apostolic mission, then the evidence of these texts suggests that that can hardly be regarded as something to be laid at the feet of Paul.

---

[1] Cf. Schüssler Fiorenza, *In Memory of Her* 167.

[2] Cf. ibid.

[3] See W. A. Meeks, *The First Urban Christians* (New Haven: Yale University, 1983) 16-19, 25-29.

[4] In the following chapter I shall discuss the view that Paul could in fact be calling here upon his own wife.

[5] Cf. Schüssler Fiorenza, *In Memory of Her* 169-70. F. X. Malinowski, 'The Brave Women of Philippi', *BTB* 15 (1985) 60-64, considers that Paul has in mind bravery and loyalty in the face of persecution, rather than direct missionary involvement.

[6] The formal partnership would be denoted by the term *koinônia/koinônein* (Phil 1:5; 4:12, 15), understood as a reference to the legal institution of the Greco-Roman world known as 'consensual *societas*'; cf. J. P. Sampley, *Pauline Partnership in Christ* (Philadelphia: Fortress, 1980) esp. pp. 51-77.

[7] Cf. Schüssler Fiorenza, *In Memory of Her* 170-71. Meeks, 'Image of the Androgyne' 198, n. 143, following A. J. Malherbe, has reservations about seeing Phoebe as an itinerant missionary; the reference may be simply to service of the church as Paul's colleague.

8   The term may even connote some exercise of authority, as in the corresponding masculine term, *prostatês*; cf. also the use of the verbal form *proistamenos* to indicate those in authority: 1 Thess 5:12; 1 Tim 3:4; 5:17. But the aspect of 'authority' can hardly be present here since Paul would hardly be describing Phoebe as one 'who presides over me'; cf. Meeks, *First Urban Christians* 60.

9   In fact, as Meeks, 'Image of the Androgyne' 198 notes, in four out of the six mentions of this couple in the New Testament Prisca's name is mentioned before that of her husband; cf. Acts 18: 2, 18, 26; Rom 16:3; 1 Cor 16:19; 2 Tim 4:19 (Aquila comes first only in the second and fifth).

10 I shall discuss this curious reference in the following chapter.

11 Cited Meeks, *First Urban Christians* 216.

12 E.g., B. Brooten, 'Junia . . . Outstanding among the Apostles', in L. and A. Swidler (eds.) *Woman Priests: A Catholic Commentary on the Vatican Declaration* (New York: Paulist, 1977) 141-44; Meeks, *First Urban Christians* 57; Schüssler Fiorenza, *In Memory of Her* 172, 201; V. Fàbrega, 'War Junia(s), der hervorragende Apostel (Rom 16,7), eine Frau?', *JahrAntChrist* 27-28 (1984-85) 47-64; earlier: M. -J. Lagrange, *Saint Paul: Épître aux Romains* (Paris: Gabalda, 1915, repr. with additions 1950) 366.

Chapter 6

Was Paul Married?

In a study enquiring into a man's attitude towards women the question as to whether he was or was not married has obvious relevance. Yet in Paul's case the issue is hardly ever raised – so prevalent and widespread is the assumption that Paul was unmarried, or that if he had been married he was certainly a widower by the time of his Christian missionary activity.[1]

That Paul was unmarried is more or less taken for granted on the basis of two references in 1 Corinthians. In 1 Cor 7:7, having given advice to married couples about living out their marriages sexually, he adds: 'I wish that all were as I myself am. But each has his own special gift (*charisma*) from God, one this way, one another'. It is generally assumed that Paul, while recognizing the validity of marriage, is expressing a wish that all shared his particular charism of celibacy. And the same thought seems to emerge from the following verse (8): 'To the unmarried and to the widows, it is a good thing for them to remain *as I am*', that is, unmarried.

The second reference that seems to ground the same assumption comes early in chapter 9. For the benefit of the Corinthians, some of whom are having difficulty putting up with the more scrupulous conscience of the weaker brethren in the matter of food (the basic issue of chapters 8-10), Paul points out that sometimes for a higher end one may choose not to exercise an acknowledged right. In illustration he points to the right, accepted in all the communities, that apostles (that is, the travelling itinerant missionaries) have a right to be supported by the local communities (v. 4). More than this, they have a right to take their wives with them and have them supported too: 'Do we not have the right to be accompanied by a (Christian) sister as wife[2] – as (is the case with) the other apostles and the brethren of the Lord and Cephas?' (v. 5). But, as he makes clear in v. 12b, so as not to put any obstacle at all in the way of the gospel, Paul has chosen not to make use of this right. That is, as generally assumed, he has foregone the right to marry.

1 Cor 7:7-8

But in neither of these two contexts is the case as open and shut as may appear at first sight. In 1 Corinthians 7, as we have argued above, the opening question is not whether one should or should not get married, but whether sexual relations even between married couples are appropriate.[3] Paul, as we have seen, while sympathetic to the Corinthians' ascetical tendencies and allowing a limited practice of abstinence, makes the full living out of married life the regular norm, lest one or other partner be tempted to seek sexual relief outside the marriage bond. Within this perspective what he says about 'desiring that all should be as I myself am' need not refer to being married or unmarried but rather to being able to live peacefully without sexual expression. Thus the *charisma* or 'gift' in v. 7b is not for Paul specifically celibacy, but that of sexual continence.[4] He is saying that some have this gift, some do not — without any suggestion that having it denotes a superior state of Christian life.

This fits in with vv. 8-9 also. His advice to the unmarried and to widows is that it is a good thing for them to be as he is — that is, to be able to live without sexual expression and so not need to be married in order to live a chaste life. But if they are not able to control their sexual desires they should marry, since it is better to marry than to be aflame with passion. This could certainly be taken to imply that Paul was unmarried. But it is also perfectly open to the possibility that he was married but lived apart from his wife, such that a more or less perpetual sexual continence was imposed upon him — a continence which he had the *charisma* to live out peaceably.

1 Cor 9:5, 12

Likewise the right that Paul refrains from exercising according to 1 Cor 9:5, 12, could certainly be the right to be married *and* to take one's spouse along with one and have her supported by the communities. But equally as well the right could simply refer to the latter two elements, that is, to take one's wife around as companion and have her supported. In this case the right to be married would simply be presupposed. Thus Paul could well be married. The right he has chosen to forego for the sake of the gospel is that of constantly being accompanied by his wife on his missionary journeys, the motive being, as the context clearly suggests, that of sparing the communities from the sort of expense that might hinder acceptance of the gospel. This would fit the picture emerging from 1 Corinthians 7 and also give us the grounds for Paul's choice of the separated life. If he does not have his wife as companion, this is not necessarily because he and his wife were not compatible. It was part of his distinctive evangelical policy of not burdening the young Gentile churches.

How fully, if such were the case, the wishes of Paul's wife entered into this apostolic decision we do not know. However, his insistence in 1 Cor 7:5 on mutuality and on the common agreement of both parties in the matter of sexual abstinence at least implies that the decision was mutual. Paul would certainly have laid himself open to the charge of hypocrisy if he commended to the Corinthians a mutuality in married life that he himself did not practise. This would be all the more embarrassing if it were publicly known that his wife begrudged her separated lot.

'Noble yokefellow' (Phil 4:3)

There is still one further text that may shed light on the matter. We have already considered Paul's call to reconciliation between two women in the community at Philippi (Phil 4:2-3). At that point I indicated the puzzle constituted by the name or title of the person called upon to effect the reconciliation. Do we have someone named 'Syzygos' – a name nowhere else attested in all extant literature? Is it part of a beneficent title, 'worthy yokefellow', addressed to an esteemed colleague? Or is the 'worthy yokefellow' in fact his own spouse? The Greek word *syzygos* is used for spouse.[5] And amongst early Christian writers no less authorities than Origen and Clement of Alexandria thought that Paul was in fact calling upon his wife at this point.[6] And while their suggestion has not generally been followed, it does have some plausibility.[7]

If there was one community where we might expect to find Paul's wife it would be that of Philippi. His correspondence with this community, recorded in Philippians, has a candour, warmth and intimacy unparalleled in the other letters. He has no complaint against them. Through moral and financial support they participated in his mission to a unique degree (cf. 4:14-20). That his wife, if such he had, should find a home among them is well conceivable.

And if his wife was a member of the community and enjoyed the status that would presumably accrue to her as his spouse, it is eminently understandable that she should be the one called upon to heal the breach between the two prominent women, Evodia and Syntyche. One might wonder why she does not feature in any greetings and why she is addressed in this formal, public way. But Philippians lacks any greetings to specific persons. To bolster her authority in the reconciliation, Paul may have let the more formal appeal stand in the letter destined to be read out publicly, while communicating privately to her in some other way.

Moreover, had Paul not married before his conversion to Jesus as the Christ, he would have been living a very anomalous life for a young Pharisee devoted to the study of the law. Jewish tradition generally and particularly the Pharisaic tradition which we find in the rabbinical literature strongly inculcated the obligation of marriage.[8] The obligation to marry was seen to stem from the prior obligation to procreate the race in fulfilment of the 'be fruitful and multiply' command of Gen 1:28. But, in a way akin to Paul's own thought in 1 Corinthians 7, there also seems to have been considerable pessimism about the ability of young men to maintain sexual purity if they were not married.[9] If Paul's adherence to the customs of his people and sect (Pharisaism) was as scrupulous as his claim in Phil 3:4-6 suggests, then we have here circumstantial evidence at least that he may in fact have married.

If Paul were in fact married, some of his utterances upon women generally and marriage specifically might be seen in a somewhat different light. Certainly, one could not lay against him the charge often laid against celibate moral theologians and legislators in the Church today, that they are giving directions in areas where they have no experience. Some might find, however, a married and separated Paul less easy to accept than a Paul who never married. Why could he and his wife not function as a missionary couple in the way that his friends Prisca and Aquila appear to have done? Perhaps Paul's mission was somewhat more mobile, more dangerous, more unsuitable for such companionship than theirs. Perhaps his wife saw her role to be somewhat different from that of Prisca. We do not know. We do not have to conclude, however, that incompatibility or inability on Paul's part to recognize woman's gifts was the reason for his separated style of life. The consuming urgency of his evangelical mission (1 Cor 9:16), the sense of all things hastening to their end (1 Cor 7:29-31): all this would account sufficiently for his marriage taking second place in his life and mission. The phenomenon is surely not unknown amongst Christian couples in past ages and today.

All this remains highly speculative and only a possibility. However, once one distances oneself imaginatively from the age-old assumption that Paul was unmarried, the hypothesis is not totally without foundation and opens up insights about Paul the man in a fresh, creative way.

---

[1] An exception is the balanced note by Yarbrough, *Not Like the Gentiles* 101, n. 34, who holds that it 'is impossible to determine whether Paul had never married or was widowed or divorced'. But for Yarbrough 1 Cor 7:8 'suggests strongly that he was not married at the time of the writing of 1 Corinthians'. Barrett, *1 Corinthians* 161, thinks it more likely that Paul was a widower; for this view see earlier, J. Jeremias, 'War Paulus Witwer?', *ZNW* 25 (1926) 310-12; idem. 'Nochmals: War Paulus Witwer?', *ZNW* 28 (1929) 321-23 (a response to a critique of the first article by E. Fascher, ibid. 62-69); P. H. Menoud, 'Marriage and Celibacy according to St. Paul' (in *Jesus Christ and the Faith: a Collection of Studies* [Pittsburgh: Pickwick, 1978] 1-18) 17, n. 10, suggests that after his conversion Paul lived apart from his wife, who remained loyal to the Jewish faith; for a similar view cf. E. Schillebeeckx: 'In all probability it was the celibacy of a man who had either left his wife or had been left by her on his conversion' (*Marriage: Secular Reality and Saving Mystery* [London: Sheed and Ward, 1965] 185-86).

[2] There has been much discussion of the curious Greek expression 'sister wife' (*gynaika adelphēn*) here. *Gûne* can mean simply woman and many older commentators, wishing to avoid the conclusion that apostles were in general married, proposed that the apostles were accompanied by 'holy women' (presumably of advanced age!) who ministered to their needs, just as it is stated of Jesus that he was accompanied by several devout women (Luke 24: 49,55). This suggestion raises more difficulties than it solves. It is far more likely that wives are meant. 'Sister' (*adelphē*) is early Christian parlance for a female fellow Christian and corresponds to the use of 'brother' (*adelphos*) for males. The combined phrase refers then to a wife who is a fellow Christian. For a useful discussion see Robertson and Plummer, *1 Corinthians* 180.

[3] See p. 19.

[4] Barrett, *1 Corinthians* 158; Yarbrough, *Not Like the Gentiles* 101.

[5] Cf. *BAG* p. 783.

[6] Ibid.

[7] The adjective 'worthy' (Gk: *gnêsios-a*) causes some difficulty here, since when referring to a wife or child it has the meaning of 'legitimate', 'true'; likewise for the feminine the usage *gnêsia* would be more normal; cf. G. Delling, *TDNT* 1.748-50. With respect to the former point, Paul's sense could be somewhat extended: 'Be a true wife to me by effecting this reconciliation . . .'.

[8] Cf. Yarbrough, *Not Like the Gentiles* 21-23; for this same reason Barrett, *1 Corinthians* 161, considers it likely that Paul was a widower.

[9] Yarbrough, ibid. 22, records the dispute amongst the rabbis as to whether one should first study Torah and then marry or whether one should study Torah having married. The issue is whether greater distraction will come from the exercise of sexual relations within marriage or from the necessity to refrain from them. In any case, as Yarbrough notes, the primary question was not whether the scholar should marry but when.

Chapter 7

The Post-Pauline Literature

Apart from the ruling about the silence of women inserted into the text of 1 Corinthians 14, most of the bad reputation attaching to Paul in the question of women rests upon statements in the 'Post-Pauline' letters. By 'Post-Pauline' I have in mind, as explained in the Introduction, the letters to the Colossians, to the Ephesians and the collection known as the Pastoral Letters (1 and 2 Timothy and Titus). With varying degrees of certainty in each case, as I shall shortly discuss, most scholars do not regard these writings as stemming directly from Paul or even from the period of his activity. In a strict sense, therefore, a case could be made out for excluding them from our consideration. However, since they went out under Paul's name and have played so prominent a part in the popular conception of his attitude to women, it is appropriate to review here what they have to say. In their own right, also, these letters cast much light on the position of women in the late New Testament period and help us see some of the reasons for the move away from the earlier equality.

Colossians

Within the body of this Post-Pauline literature Colossians and Ephesians stand rather much together. But Colossians has a far stronger claim to authorship by Paul, since in shape and content it still has much in common with the genuinely Pauline letters. But a much more elaborate style and some key differences in content (in the areas, especially, of christology, eschatology, church, ministry and baptism) have persuaded most scholars that the letter has been written by a disciple of Paul, possibly within a decade of the apostle's death.[1] The purpose of the letter is to counter false doctrine, showing itself in the worship of angels, seen as having a constituent role in the universe. Against this the writer asserts the unique role and supremacy of Christ in the work of universal reconciliation.

We have noted that in the exhortation to the Christian life making up its latter half, Colossians has an echo of the baptismal formula quoted in Gal 3:28 (Col 3:11) — but without the 'male/ female' element and with a considerable loosening of the overall construction. Later on the exhortation becomes far more specific in the shape of a distinctive ethical form known as a *household code*. The household code regulated domestic relationships in the three key areas: wives/husbands; children/parents; slaves/masters. Examples of this code are found across the later New Testament letters: Col 3:18 – 4:2; Eph 5:21 – 6:9; 1 Tim 2:8-15; 5:1-2; 6:1-2; Tit 2:1-10; 3:1; 1 Pet 2:18-25; 3:1-7). The code was not specifically Christian; in fact, along with similar examples in Hellenistic Jewish literature, it essentially reflects the patriarchal ethic of the Greco-Roman household.[2] In the three social relationships mentioned above it urged submissiveness on the part of the 'inferior' member (wife, child, slave) and kindness, reasonableness on the part of the 'superior' (husband, parent, master). In this way it sought to promote the domestic harmony and stability which were widely regarded throughout the ancient world as the basis of political and social peace.

In Colossians 3 we have the earliest and most complete example of the household code in the New Testament:

[18]Wives, be subject to your husbands, as is fitting in the Lord;
[19]Husbands, love your wives, and do not be harsh with them.
[20]Children, obey your parents in everything . . .
[21]Fathers, do not provoke your children . . .
[22-25]Slaves, obey in everything those who are your earthly masters . . .
[4:1]Masters, treat your slaves justly and fairly . . .

Though I have not quoted it in full, we may note that the exhortation to slaves to be obedient (vv. 22-25) is developed here beyond all proportion in comparison with the rest. Clearly, it is this relationship that is of primary concern to the author. The remaining exhortations are fairly conventional, each one being given a religious basis through some reference to the Lord. Whereas children and slaves are urged to 'be obedient' (Gk: *hypakouein*), wives are required to 'be subject' (*hypotassesthai* — the same expression as in 1 Cor 14:34). This is said to be 'fitting in the Lord' — a far cry from the basic equality of man and woman 'in the Lord' of 1 Cor 11:11. What has replaced this equality is the 'love-patriarchalism' expressed in the corresponding exhortation to the husbands – to love their wives and not treat them harshly.[3] The basis of woman's position and treatment is no longer her equal status and dignity, as in 1 Corinthians 7, but the love and benevolence of her husband – conditioned no doubt in many instances by her own readiness to be submissive.

Ephesians

The reasons for this shift away from equality in relationships between husband and wife to the 'love-patriarchalism' of the household code we shall explore later on. In the meantime let us note the rather different version of the household code found in Ephesians. Whereas Colossians stands close to the period of the genuine Pauline letters, Ephesians represents a systematic reflection upon the vocation and achievement of Paul from a far greater distance. The union of Jew and Gentile within the Church is now an accomplished fact. The writer meditates upon this mighty achievement of God's power in order to hold out the possibility of an even greater reconciliation – the unification of the entire universe through the on-going work of God in Christ, manifested in the Church.

Ephesians obviously takes Colossians as its model in many respects, developing even further the ideas of reconciliation and church. In its exhortatory section it features a developed form of the household code (5:21 – 6:9). In contrast to Colossians, the element dealing with husband/wife relationships (5:21-33) is considerably expanded:

[21]Be subject to one another out of reverence for Christ:
[22]wives, to your husbands, as to the Lord. [23]For the husband is the head of the wife as Christ is the head of the church, his body, and is himself its Saviour. [24]But as the church is subject to Christ, so wives in everything to their husbands.
[25]Husbands, love your wives, as Christ loved the church and gave himself up for her, [26]that he might sanctify her, having cleansed her by the washing of water with the word, [27]that he might present the church to himself in splendour, without spot or wrinkle or any such thing, that she might be holy and without blemish. [28]Even so husbands should love their wives as their own bodies. He who loves his wife loves himself. [29]For no man ever hates his own flesh, but nourishes and cherishes it, as Christ does the church, [30]because we are members of his body. [31]For this reason a man shall leave his father and mother and be joined to his wife, and the two shall become one. [32]This is a great mystery, and I mean in reference to Christ and the church;

[33]however, let each one of you love his wife as himself, and let the wife see that she respects her husband.

At first sight this passage appears to place Christian wives in an extremely subordinationist position – and, moreover, to cement that position theologically by comparing the husband/wife relationship to that existing between Christ and the church. It is true that a subordinate role is assigned to wives here. But matters are not so simple and several details in the passage call for closer inspection.

In the first place the call for wives to be subject in vv. 22-24 is prefaced by the more general summons to all Christians to 'be subject to one another out of reverence for Christ' stated in v. 21.[4] Thus the specific calls for subjection in the following household code, including that addressed to the wives, are placed within the call to mutual subjection incumbent upon all Christians, who must see and reverence Christ in one another.[5] Even the subsequent call to husbands to 'love their wives' (v. 25) would seem to be included under the general Christian rubric of reverential subjection to the interests of the other (cf. Phil 2:1-5).

Secondly and more importantly, the idea of subjection on the part of the woman does not rest, as so commonly thought, on the fact that the husband is said to be the 'head' of the woman, as Christ is the head of the church (vv. 23-24). The basis of this misconception is the understanding of 'head' here in the metaphorical sense, perfectly legitimate in English, as 'superior'.[6] But, as we have already seen in connection with 1 Cor 11:2-16, 'head' (*kephalē*) does not have this sense in Greek – neither secular nor New Testament Greek.[7] The most suitable New Testament metaphorical understanding is that of 'source' – and this certainly fits the other two places in Ephesians (1:22 and 4:15) where the word is used, in each case with respect to Christ's headship of the church.[8] Notice that here too, immediately after the statement that Christ is the church's head there follows the explanation, '(for) he himself is the saviour of the body'. It is not, then, as its superior that Christ is the 'head' of the church in Ephesians.[9] He is 'head' as the source of its life, as the one who gave himself up for it (v. 25), who nourishes it and performs all the other services listed later on within the nuptial image. It is this sense of headship which the analogy of Christ and the church conveys to the relationship between husband and wife. The analogy is not to be pressed in all details – clearly the husband is not to be understood as the 'saviour' of the wife.[10] But the wife sees in the husband the one who cherishes, supports and gives himself for her. Her submission, her 'being subject', is a response to this loving care. In the end, it is true, she submits to his authority. But what prompts this is his love – rather than that simply in the nature of things he has authority over her.

The bulk of the exhortation, however, is addressed to husbands (vv. 25-32), with considerable enlargement of the analogy of Christ in relation to the church. The development continues to spell out what being 'head' involves, though the further metaphors of 'betrothal' and 'bridal presentation' (seemingly based upon Paul's image in 2 Cor 11:2) enter in. In the end what began as the analogy (Christ's relationship to the church) seems to take over and become the main focus of interest. To justify the idea that in loving his wife the husband loves 'his own flesh' the author cites Gen 2:24 which speaks of a man leaving his father and mother and becoming joined to his wife so that the two become one flesh. The rabbis saw in this text Scripture's attestation of the sacredness of marriage. The author of Ephesians, however, goes one step further. By seeing here a 'great mystery' (v. 32) he finds in the Genesis text a hidden meaning that is only now (that is, eschatologically) understood: the text spoke of the sacred nature of marriage, but in so doing it foreshadowed a deeper mystery, the relationship between Christ and the church.[11] In this sacramental way the two relationships mutually illuminate one another. Returning, however, to the moral instruction which is his primary concern, the author concludes (v. 33), as he began, with a dual exhortation addressed to both husband and wife: each husband is to love his wife as he loves himself, the wife is to see that she reverences her husband.

It should be clear, then, that though the wife is urged to be subject to her husband, the basis for this is the mutual love and respect between each other as Christians. Elisabeth Schüssler Fiorenza acknowledges that through the introduction of the analogy drawn from the relationship between Christ and the church the patriarchal household code in Ephesians undergoes essential modification and is indeed radically questioned.[12] However, in her view the christological modification stressing the primacy of love and service is not strong enough to transform the patriarchal pattern; instead, 'Ephesians christologically cements the inferior position of the wife in the marriage relationship'.[13] This may well have been the actual effect of the text of Ephesians. Certainly, a relationship of equality between husband and wife could hardly emerge from the 'Christchurch' analogy. However, one may question whether the inequality aspect need have found such reinforcement had 'headship' not been understood primarily in terms of authority. It is natural, granted modern usage, that such an understanding should prevail. But, as I have argued above, that was probably not the original meaning and it should certainly not determine the matter today.

The Pastoral Letters

The three letters 1 and 2 Timothy and Titus are recognized by virtually all scholars as written in the name of Paul by an unknown Christian around the turn of the first century.[14] Though purporting to be letters, and cast in this form, they are actually manifestos concerned with the preservation of sound teaching in the face of disturbing new ideas, which seem to have considerable affinity to later Gnostic doctrine.[15] To counter this threat the author is much preoccupied with the governance of the church. He is particularly anxious that sound, responsible and reputable officials be appointed and that the rest of the faithful give them due respect.

The letters are aptly called 'Pastoral' because they are not so much concerned with the mission to non-believers as with the proper ordering of existing communities and with the ability of these communities to live in peace and respectability in the surrounding non-believing world. In these letters the household code, which earlier regulated relationships between specific groups within the community, has now become the model of the entire church – the 'household of God' (1 Tim 3:15). Before the outside world the church must present the image of a well-governed, peaceful household, presided over by the presbyter-bishop, to whom as *paterfamilias* all give obedience and respect.

These three letters are written in Paul's name.[16] Perhaps at the time of the publication and diffusion of the genuine letters a Christian leader, whose own links to Paul may have been quite remote, sought to enlist the authority of the Apostle for the order he wished to foster. Though the letters contain several echoes of Paul's teaching and presuppose his authority as a living force, they belong really to a vastly different world and may not even stem from communities directly founded by him. What they say about women should not, then, immediately be laid at Paul's door. In fact, in many instances, as we shall see, their recommendations and interpretations are considerably at variance with his own thought.

The letters do contain a number of references to women and in this sense they convey a good deal of information about women's status and role in the church of the time, even when seeking to curtail or regulate it.[17] The instruction on deacons in 1 Tim 3:8-13 seems to presuppose a female group of deacons in parallel to the male deacons. The instruction that the women 'be serious, not slanderers, but temperate, faithful in all things' (v. 11) simply echoes what is required of the men.

Nonetheless, there seems to be a concerted effort to suppress expectations on the part of women to have a more significant part in community life, expectations which may have survived from the earlier period of equality. Notorious in this context is the text from 1 Tim 2:8-15. We have already cited this when seeking a context for the ruling inserted into 1 Cor 14:33-36. However, it bears closer inspection:

> [8]I desire that in every place when praying the men should lift holy hands without anger or quarrelling; [9]and that the women should do likewise[18] in modest deportment, decking themselves out with chastity and prudence, not with braided hair or gold or pearls or costly attire [10]but with good deeds, as befits women who profess religion. [11]Let a woman learn in silence with all submissiveness. [12]I permit no woman to teach or to have authority over men; she is to keep silent. [13]For Adam was formed first, then Eve; [14]and Adam was not deceived, but the woman was deceived and became a transgressor. [15]Yet woman will be saved through bearing children, if she continues in faith and love and holiness, with modesty.

The overall context of this passage is an instruction concerning public prayer, beginning with the indication in 2:1-2 of persons who are to be prayed for (notably civic authorities, 'that we may lead a quiet and peaceable life'). After something of a digression in vv. 3-7, the author, mentioning first the men, then the women, speaks of essential conditions that must accompany the prayer. The men should lift holy hands without anger or quarreling (v. 8); the women should be adorned with chastity and prudence, rather than with braided hair, precious stones or costly attire (vv. 9-10).

Note that these latter verses do not contain a directive concerning what women should wear, neither in general nor in the more specific context of worship.[19] The whole subject of female attire is used metaphorically to refer to the virtues with which the women should be clad when the community comes together for prayer. The virtues of modesty and chastity take the place in the Christian assembly of elaborate coiffure and costly adornment.[20] Thus the exhortation is to virtue in general. It is not a ruling on what women should wear. Moreover, the text does seem to presume that women, along with the men, took part in public prayer.

The second part of this instruction (vv. 11-15) seems to conflict with this latter point in that it enjoins silence upon women in the public assembly.[21] But what it forbids is not any kind of utterance but women presuming to teach, something that goes beyond simple prayer. The writer has two grounds for this ban. In the first place, were women to teach it would imply that they had authority over men (v. 12) which is contrary to the order of creation where Adam was created before Eve (v. 13). Secondly — and perhaps most offensively of all — the biblical account of the Fall (Genesis 3), which speaks of Eve's deception and lapse into transgression, is taken as indicating the general unreliability of women: like the gullible Eve they cannot be trusted to teach.[22]

The first argument from priority of creation has clear affinities to that deployed by Paul in 1 Cor 11:8-9 (countermanded to some extent by vv. 11-12 in the same passage). The second has some foreshadowing in 2 Cor 11:2: 'But I am afraid that as the serpent deceived Eve by his cunning, your thoughts will be led astray from a sincere and pure devotion to Christ'. But where Paul applies the possibility of an Eve-like deception to the entire (male and female) community at Corinth, the author of the present text makes it apply narrowly and brutally to women alone. Paul may recognize the deception of Eve, but for him Adam remains the archetypal sinner. The unfortunate interpretation of Genesis 3 which features here is hardly a development of his own thought.[23] It has more in common with misogynist interpretations of Genesis 3 to be found in certain Jewish and later Christian texts where Eve takes the entire blame, with Adam being let off more or less scot free.[24]

The final statement in this text to the effect that woman 'will be saved through childbearing' (v. 15) probably again derives from the account of the Fall in Genesis 3, specifically from the reference to childbirth in 3:16 ('in pain you shall bring forth your children'). Woman will achieve salvation not through taking on masculine roles such as teaching but through the task clearly appointed to her in Scripture: bearing children.

At this point we might recall that Paul throughout his lengthy discussion of the relationship between husband and wife in marriage in 1 Corinthians 7 never mentions this function. On the contrary his preference for celibacy tended to relieve woman of the obligation to bear children, which was pressed upon her so insistently by the surrounding culture.[25] Here again, then, is a clear case where the author of the Pastorals restores the traditional conventional role, giving it a vaguely Christian colouring by means of the concluding proviso about 'continuing in faith, love and holiness with modesty'.

Such teaching role as the author of the Pastorals concedes to women is restricted to their teaching other women. Even then it is simply a matter of the older women teaching the younger ones the true womanly virtues, as he conceives these to be (Tit 2:3-5):

> [3]In the same way bid the older women to be reverent in their conduct, not given to gossip or slaves to much drink, teachers of good things, [4]so that they can train the young women to be lovers of their husbands, lovers of their children, [5]to be sensible, pure, fulfillers of their household duties and submissive to their husbands, so that the word of God may not be brought into disrepute.

Here we have the complete reassertion of the domestic role of women as in the traditional household codes. And, apart from the internal order of the community, the overriding motive – as also in the case of the instructions concerning younger men (cf. v. 8) – is the good reputation of the community amongst outsiders.

A similar tone pervades the rather lengthy instruction in 1 Timothy 5 concerning widows. The biblical tradition generally regarded care of the defenceless widow as a particular community responsibility. This continued in early Christianity, but as well as receiving support, the widows seem to have constituted a special group themselves occupied in deeds of kindness and hospitality (cf. Acts 6:1; 9:36-41). 1 Tim 5:3-16 shows that this institution was alive and vigorous in the community addressed by the Pastorals.[26] The author, however, wishes to regulate this institution and curb certain abuses. He is particularly concerned that only really needy and deserving widows be listed for support – those who have families to support them should not be enrolled (vv. 4-8). He is also anxious that young widows not be enrolled: they tend after a while to want to re-marry and so abandon their pledge (not to re-marry); they become restless and 'learn to be idlers, gadding about from house to house, and not only idlers but gossips and busy-bodies, saying what they should not' (v. 13). The writer may be speaking from experience, but once more we seem to have reappearing the misogynist view never far from the surface. The writer wants these younger widows to 'marry, bear children, rule their households, and give the enemy no occasion to revile us' (v. 14). Here again are the positive virtues of the household code, with the prevailing motivation — the good repute of the church. In a hostile and suspicious world the community must be blameless examples of the household virtues which that world held in highest regard.

Some indication of what the author may have been up against in trying to restore women in the community to a more conventional place is provided by literature suggesting that in some circles women continued to exercise preaching and teaching roles. Thus the author of Revelation (the Apocalypse) takes the 'angel' of the church at Thyatira to task for tolerating 'the woman Jezebel, who calls herself a prophetess and is teaching and beguiling my servants to practise immorality' (2:20). More striking, however, is the figure of Thecla depicted in the non-canonical second century work, the *Acts of Paul and Thecla*.[27] Thecla is presented as a missionary companion of Paul, working in close attachment to him but under a vow of continence. Interestingly enough in view of tendencies in the Corinthian congregation reflected in 1 Corinthians 11, she is said to have shorn her hair and gone about in men's clothing. In this she may illustrate the Gnostic aspiration to overcome the male-female dichotomy by assimilating the female to the male. In any case Thecla was regarded by later writers such as Tertullian as a kind of archetypal female teacher and preacher, whose story was cited in justification of woman's right to hold such roles within the community.[28]

It seems highly likely that Christian women aspiring to fulfil these roles found sympathy and support in circles tending in the Gnostic direction which the author of the Pastoral Letters was combatting.[29] The specific complaint recorded in 2 Tim 3:6-7 about men who 'make their way into households and capture weak women, burdened with sins and swayed by various impulses who are always studying but never able to arrive at a knowledge of the truth' may allude to the attraction such teachings held for women.[30] The attempt to restore women to their household duties and prevent them from teaching is, then, part and parcel of the author's overall campaign to counter such tendencies in order to preserve the integrity of the church and its acceptance in the wider society. We may regret the effect such texts have had in Christian history, especially when they have gone out in Paul's name and authority. But a critical use of the Bible will also strive to relate them to the challenges and difficulties faced by the communities from which they sprang and to which they were addressed.[31]

Conclusion

Looking back over the Post-Pauline literature which we have surveyed for its statements concerning women, we can see the dominance of the household code. This makes its first appearance, as we have seen, in Colossians and steadily becomes more determinative until in the Pastoral Letters it has become the controlling image of the church itself. As the Christian communities became more noticeable in wider Greco-Roman society, the condition for their survival was that they cease to appear as just another of the much criticized eastern cults, with a social and familial ethos standing in radical challenge to that of the surrounding world. Without surrendering essential values, they had to present themselves as embodying all that seemed best in social terms to that world. Thus the radical, world-challenging proclamation of equality in Gal 3:28 gave way to the sober domesticity of the household codes. At the same time the very literature that promotes that domesticity also sheds light on the extreme extension of the radical, world-denying tendencies to be found in the counter movement. In what the author of the Pastoral Letters is combatting we may well have the tendencies that made Paul nervous in Corinth come to full term.

At stake in the conflict was nothing less than the ability of the church to relate creatively to the surrounding world, which — contrary to the earlier apocalyptic view — was clearly going to be around for a long time. Upon this possibility hung the very survival of the Christian movement as something other than a world-denying Gnostic sect. There was a price to be paid in all this, a measure of compromise with the values of that world, especially in the areas represented by the code. The compromise on women, along with that on slavery, was part of that price. We may consider the price too high. We may deplore the continuing effects. But if we are to deal creatively with this legacy, it will help to understand the circumstances towards the end of the first century that occasioned its birth.

1 For discussion of the question see esp. W. G. Kümmel, *Introduction to the New Testament* (rev. ed.; London: SCM, 1975) 340-46 (concluding to authenticity); N. Perrin and D. C. Duling, *The New Testament: An Introduction* (2d ed.; New York, etc.: Harcourt, Brace, Jovanovich, 1982) 210-12 (concluding to non-authenticity). See also M. Kiley, *Colossians as Pseudepigraphy* (Sheffield: JSOT, 1986), which discusses the authorship of Colossians within the wider context of the phenomenon of pseudepigraphical writing in the Greco-Roman world (see esp. pp. 15-35). In the case of Colossians and Ephesians, however, it may be more appropriate to avoid the term 'pseudepigraphy' (that is, writing under an assumed name, whether this 'fiction' is known to the readers or not) and to speak instead of 'extended authorship', which occurs when after the death of a teacher one or more of his disciples write in his name, developing and interpreting his original doctrine; for the latter phrase and definition I am indebted to the very helpful essay by my colleague W. J. Dalton, 'Pseudepigraphy in the New Testament', *Catholic Theological Review* (Melbourne) 5 (1983) 29-35, see esp. p. 32.

2 For a most comprehensive recent discussion of the origin of the household code see D. L. Balch, *Let Wives Be Submissive: The Domestic Code in 1 Peter* (SBLMS 26; Chico, CA: Scholars, 1981).

3 On 'love-patriarchalism' see G. Theissen, *The Social Setting of Pauline Christianity* (Philadelphia: Fortress, 1982) 107-110; Schüssler Fiorenza, *In Memory of Her* 78-80.

4 Most English translations (e.g., RSV, Jerusalem Bible), for clarity's sake, begin a new paragraph at the beginning of v. 21. But in the Greek the verse consists simply of a participial phrase tacked on to the preceding more general exhortation, which suggests that the statement in v. 21 is very much meant to be read as a bridge between the two sections.

5 Cf. M. Barth, *Ephesians 4-6* (AB 34 A; New York: Doubleday, 1979) 610-11.

6 As, e.g., by J. R. Sampley, *'And the Two shall become One Flesh': A Study of Traditions in Ephesians 5:21-33* (Cambridge: Cambridge University, 1971) 123-23.

7 See esp. Murphy-O'Connor, 'Sex and Logic' 491-93 and pp. 41-42 above.

8 Cf. esp. 4:15-16: '. . . we are to grow up in every way into him who is the head, into Christ, 16from whom the whole body, joined and knit together by every joint with which it is supplied, when each part is working properly, makes bodily growth and builds itself up in love' (RSV).

9 As Sampley, *'And the Two shall become One Flesh'* 123-24.

10 Allowing for the necessary differences between the two relationships is the reason for the strong adversative 'but' (Gk *alla*) standing at the beginning of v. 24. The sense is then: '(The difference notwithstanding) just as the church submits herself . . .'; cf. Barth, *Ephesians 4-6* 619; also M. Evans, *Woman in the Bible* (Exeter: Paternoster, 1983) 74-75.

11 Cf. J. A. Grassi, 'The Letter to the Ephesians' in *JBC* 2.341-49, esp. 349a; Sampley, *'And the Two shall become One Flesh'* 94-96.

12 *In Memory of Her* 269-70.

13 Ibid. 270.

14 The reasons for this judgement are extensively set out by Kümmel, *Introduction to the New Testament* 370-84

15 Cf. Perrin and Duling, *New Testament Introduction* 385, 388-90.

16 Cf. Dalton, 'Pseudepigraphy' 33: '. . . the Pastoral Letters are examples of real pseudepigraphy, by which a later writer, with good conscience and for the good of the church, succeeded in persuading his readers that these letters really came from Paul'.

17 For the reconstruction see esp. Schüssler Fiorenza, *In Memory of Her* 288-91; 309-13.

[18] This translation brings out properly the parallel between what is required of the men and what of the women, as suggested by the Greek conjunction *hôsautôs*: both situations have to do with the moral probity that should accompany prayer; cf. M. Dibelius and H. Conzelmann, *The Pastoral Epistles* (Hermeneia; Philadelphia: Fortress, 1972) 45.

[19] As J. N. D. Kelly, *The Pastoral Epistles* (London: Black, 1963) 66.

[20] Cf. Dibelius and Conzelmann: 'The accent in the Pastorals lies not in the idea that women should (modestly!) adorn themselves, but rather that true ornamentation is not external at all' (*The Pastoral Epistles* 46).

[21] The Greek word *hêsychia* can also mean keeping quiet or still, as well as keeping silence and some (e.g., Schüssler Fiorenza, *In Memory of Her* 290, 335) see here simply an injunction to quiet behaviour. But the explicit contrast with the prohibition on public teaching suggests that actual silence rather than simply quietness is what is being commanded.

[22] Cf. Kelly, *Pastoral Epistles* 68-69.

[23] Schüssler Fiorenza, *In Memory of Her* 235, acknowledges the difference between 2 Cor 11:3 and the present text, but nevertheless holds that Paul, by employing the metaphor of the virgin-bride and seeing the church in danger, like Eve, of being seduced, opened the door to the later subordinationist applications.

[24] E.g. Sir 25:24: 'The beginning of sin was by the woman; and through her we all die'; cf. Adam & Eve 10:3-4; 16:3; 33:1-3; 35:3 (= Apoc Moses 9:2) 38:1-2 (= Apoc Moses 11:1-2); 44:2 (= Apoc Moses 14:2); Apoc Moses 15-21; 1 Enoch 69:6-7; 2 Enoch 31:6. Christian developments of this theme can be found in Pseudo-Clementine literature.

[25] Cf. Schüssler Fiorenza, *In Memory of Her* 224-26; Yarbrough, *Not Like the Gentiles* 45-46, 60-62.

[26] I am not persuaded that 1 Tim 5:3-16 provides evidence that widows, in addition to their charitable functions 'had leadership positions similar to those of the bishop', as Schüssler Fiorenza, *In Memory of Her* 310, maintains.

[27] English translation in E. Hennecke, *New Testament Apocrypha* (ed. W. Schneemelcher; 2 vols.; London: Lutterworth, 1963, 1965) 2.353-64. For a sympathetic account of Thecla, see Schüssler Fiorenza, *In Memory of Her* 173-75.

[28] Cf. R. Scroggs, 'Woman in the NT', *IDBSupp* 966-968, esp. 968.

[29] It is generally accepted that in Gnostic communities women enjoyed more prominent roles and positions than they did in orthodox circles. E. H. Pagels has argued that it was because of the pre-eminent status it accorded to women that orthodox Christians branded Gnosticism as a heresy and sought vigorously to suppress it – whereas in fact the Gnostics in this respect were only preserving values of early Christianity (e.g. those in Gal 3:28) from which orthodoxy had deviated (*The Gnostic Gospels* [New York: Random House, 1979]) 57-69. But this thesis has been criticized by other writers, who point out the fundamentally patriarchalist tendencies of Gnosticism (e.g., the absorption of the female into the male) and note also the many other features (contempt for the world and for the body, elitism, dualism) which made for its rejection; see Schüssler Fiorenza, *In Memory of Her* 274-75; S. Heine, *Women and Early Christianity* (London: SCM, 1987) 107-34, 141-46.

[30] Cf. Schüssler Fiorenza, *In Memory of Her* 312.

[31] For a notably balanced assessment of the continuing significance of the Pastoral Letters see R. Brown, *The Churches the Apostles Left Behind* (New York: Paulist, 1984), chapter 2 (pp. 31-46).

Concluding Reflections

We have completed our survey of the Pauline material on women. As I said at the start, it was not my intention to defend Paul at all costs. If, however, the interpretations I have presented for the texts that do seem to stem from his pen (as distinct from those written later in his name) stand up, then perhaps Paul himself can be freed from much blame. Moreover, the study of the texts within their context and the better appreciation of the circumstances — pastoral, social, theological — that gave rise to them may in fact lead to a judgment that within those circumstances Paul did not totally lay his creativity aside when dealing with this issue.

At the same time an observation made by D. R. MacDonald with respect to Gal 3:28 can probably be extended across the whole issue of Paul and women. To seek to find in Paul a 'quondam feminist' is

> to commit a chronological injustice, for it wrongly extradites Paul from his world and places him on trial in our own. We must allow him to return to the first century, and judge him in the light of the problems and presuppositions of that age.[1]

That is precisely what I have been trying to do.

But whatever about Paul and his own intentions, the effect down the centuries of what has gone out in his name stands. That the Pauline writings have reinforced and continue to reinforce androcentric tendencies cannot be denied.

It does help to distinguish Paul from the subsequent effect of his writings. It is also important to recognize what is 'authentic' Paul and what 'inauthentic' in the sense of being composed by later writers in his name. The authority of the Apostle should not be invoked over the later writings — even though the post-Pauline material remains Scripture and doubtless in many circles will continue to be attributed to Paul.

Using Scripture today: Word and Spirit

What matters above all, surely, is the *use* made of Scripture in church life and practice. There is a temptation to look to Scripture for a blueprint for church life and structure for all time. The Pauline writings are particularly susceptible to this because in them one finds not only much information about the life of the early communities but also a great many directives concerning the shape it should take. The kind of investigation undertaken in this study, however, always trying to see a text within its literary and circumstantial context, should put us on guard against literalist interpretations of this kind.

Paul wrote to fledgling communities whose grasp of the gospel was anything but complete. Their Christian life was still very much evolving in interaction and dialogue with influences from within and from without — the advent of new teachers like Apollos at Corinth, for example, and the temptations and opportunities presented by the non-believing world. We now recognize that even his seemingly more 'systematic' writings, such as Romans, were in fact highly determined by the particular situation to which they were addressed. There is something bizarre, then, in erecting into rules for all time the very much time and circumstance bound directives Paul addressed to specific situations. Were he to find us doing so twenty centuries later, his surprise and embarrassment would doubtless be acute.

Moreover, as well as looking at circumstances in New Testament community life, we have to read each passage in its own literary context — to discern the flow of argument, to see what was the primary intention and what served simply as support along the way. Thus, to take Paul's remark in 1 Cor 11:7-9 that man is the image and glory of God whereas woman is simply the glory of man and use this observation to debar woman from sacramental office because she cannot image God, is to proceed in a fundamentalist way completely insensitive to the nature of a text. It is to fail to notice that Paul immediately (vv. 11-12) 'corrects' the subordinationism implicit in this argument and in the end, having gained his practical conclusion, virtually throws the argument itself away. It would be curious that we should dismiss the practical ruling (the wearing of veils) — about which Paul cared a very great deal — and take with great seriousness and extend even wider the arguments Paul used to get to that ruling, arguments whose weakness he himself sensed keenly.[2]

Paul himself gives us a guide for the proper use of Scripture in his own procedure in Galatians. In that letter, as we have seen, he recalls the Galatian community to their own experience of the Spirit and then takes them on a lengthy reading of the Scriptures in the light of the Spirit. In the interplay of Scripture and Spirit God's present will for the community is discerned. To read Scripture apart from the Spirit moving in the community is to render it 'Letter' and, as he remarks chillingly in another place (2 Cor 3:6b), 'The letter kills; whereas the Spirit gives life'. 'Letter' for Paul reduces Scripture to the arid legalism that he identifies with the Old Age — the epoch characterized by sin, slavery and alienation from God.

Christian freedom

Thus a reading of Scripture that is not fundamentally liberating is a reading untrue to Paul. To read the Scripture in the Spirit is always to be set free, for, as Paul again remarks, the index of the Spirit is freedom: 'Where the Spirit of the Lord is, there is freedom' (2 Cor 3:17). This is the eschatological freedom of the children of God, about which Paul speaks so much in Galatians and Romans 8. It is the freedom 'associated with the glory of the children of God' (Rom 8:21); it attends the arrival of men and women at the goal intended by God for the human race from the start: the fullness of humanity already seen in the Risen Jesus (Rom 8:29-30).

The gospel, then, is always a proclamation of freedom. This is clear in its key Old Testament archetypes and foreshadowings: the Exodus liberation from Egyptian slavery and the New Exodus from Babylonian Exile proclaimed by Second Isaiah (Isaiah 40-66). Freedom — from disease, hunger, demonic possession, the grip of guilt and ignorance — is also the effect of Jesus' proclamation and actualisation of the 'Kingdom' in the Synoptic Gospels. In the Fourth Gospel it is the product of the 'truth' revealed by the Son of God (8:31-36).

But the fostering and preservation of Christian freedom is a subtle thing. And none knows this better than Paul. He calls upon the Galatians to stand firm in the 'freedom with which Christ has set us free' (5:1). Very soon, however, he urges them not to allow their freedom to provide an opportunity 'for the flesh', that is for the basic human tendency to selfishness that can poison community life even in the New Age.

The Corinthian women who removed their veils doubtless saw in this a gesture of freedom – an exercise of the *exousia* that Paul had taught them attended their new existence in the Lord, a living out of the baptismal freedom proclaimed in Gal 3:28. Paul, however, took a different view. In this there may have been an element of neurotic prejudice and fear. On the other hand in the knowledge of tendencies in Corinth leading to the Gnostic path it may *for its time* have been a directive well-founded in its pastoral concern.

A liberating reading of Scripture

This enquiry began with a study of Paul's letter to the Galatians. We reviewed there his summons to the Galatian Christians to stand firm in the freedom Christ had won for them and not seek to go back to the slavery of the former age. Central to that summons was a Spirit-filled reading of Scripture, a discovery in it of gospel, not law. The question for us today is basically the same: whether we will allow the texts to imprison us or free us, to stand as gospel or as law. Certainly they do not relieve us of the painful responsibility of discerning as a community enlightened by the Spirit their true meaning as Scripture for today.

In this the 'difficult' post-Pauline texts may, paradoxically, have a special role. As we have seen, the far more restrictive attitude towards Christian woman reflected in these writings stemmed basically from two causes: the struggle against Gnosticism and the attempt to survive as a religious movement in a hostile world once the 'umbrella' of Judaism had been removed. The former (Gnosticism) seemed to offer women a greater freedom, true to the original equality proclaimed in Gal 3:28. Ultimately, however, that freedom was illusory since it could not relate positively to life in the body, to the material world and to the rest of the faithful. The second factor, the need to gain some respectability before the outside world was the condition not only for survival but also for mission: for 'holding out to the world the life-giving word' of Christ (cf. Phil 2:16). Before we judge too harshly the compromises, the oppressions reflected in these texts we should look at the pattern of church history, at the compromises and adaptations to the world that have marked its flow down to and including our own day. Never since Pentecost has a completely 'pure' distillation of the gospel essence been anywhere manifest in Christian community life.

What is surely the task of present-day Christians, reading the Scriptures in the light of the Spirit, is to discern the appropriate shape of church structure today. In this tradition will also have its part – as it did for Paul (cf.1 Cor 11:2,16)![3] For tradition as well as Scripture shapes identity and, even in more practical aspects, cannot lightly be set aside. The pain, the dislocation, the loss suffered in the Catholic Church as a result of the rapid and ill-explained liturgical change following Vatican II is a clear lesson in this. Anthropologists rather than theologians should perhaps be given the final say. But a tradition kept simply for its own sake, unexamined, unrevised, may cease to communicate life and freedom. If it alienates a body of the faithful, if its scriptural foundation is dubious or reflective of circumstances that no longer apply, if it does not equip the community for mission, then its essential tie to the core of the gospel must be questioned.

Women in the church

To speak more explicitly, if the directions concerning women in the Pauline texts are seen to reflect social situations no longer truly applicable, then those directives should no longer be heeded as, literally, 'holy Scripture'. We may continue to read them out. But if we do we should read them with advertence to their context and to the fact that Scripture is always a human expression of the word of God.[4] We should see in them the ways in which the Church in its formative period adapted the values of Jesus to the circumstances, threats and opportunities of its time. We should find in this, not law, not imprisonment, but instruction – perhaps warning too – about what is incumbent upon believers in our time.

Many people, I know, will pick up this book with the question of woman's ordination foremost in their mind. If I have said nothing explicit on this matter so far, it is because I believe that the Pauline texts do not bear immediately upon it. Certainly they are often invoked to forbid it. But the whole examination entered upon here may serve to show that I do not believe such conclusions can legitimately be drawn. Whether Paul, rightly interpreted, points directly in the opposite direction is a more complex matter. Certainly the statement of equality preserved from an early period in the fragment of Gal 3:28 remains a challenge to present structures — especially if it stands in continuity with attitudes and stances taken towards women by Jesus himself. In fact, the more one charts in the New Testament texts the relentless drift towards the dominance of men, the more one comes to appreciate what a mighty impulse in the opposite direction the Christian movement must have received in its beginnings — an impulse from Jesus which the later records never quite managed to obscure.

What the subsequent texts, Pauline and post-Pauline, show is the task and the difficulty of embodying the values of Jesus when circumstances and community life have changed. Our generation, too, must carry on the labour, the discernment that Paul and the early Christians before him began. Part of that discernment of the Spirit will doubtless be no small measure of dialogue, conflict and pain. The whole story of Jesus shows that freedom, growth, true humanity is not won without cost — even if God's grace is free.

But the scriptural texts, including the Pauline ones, can only be one element in the whole process. The key thing is to ensure that they function as gospel, not as law, that they open up new visions rather than encasing old ones, that they work towards the ever fuller realization of God's plan for human beings sketched in Gen 1:26-27 and brought to fulfilment in Christ according to Gal 3:28.

If 'in Christ', alongside the 'neither Jew nor Greek, slave nor free', there is also 'no male and female', then there is a sense in which the Risen Jesus transcends the 'maleness' of his historical existence and becomes one in whom all believers should feel equally at home. That the Church, the 'body' of the Risen Lord, should reflect this availability seems both appropriate and true. There is a sense, then, in which Gal 3:28 remains for this issue both Paul's first and his final word — the implications for our own time we are perhaps only beginning to understand.

---

[1] *No Male and Female* 130.

[2] Cf. J. P. Meier's telling comparison, 'Veiling of Hermeneutics' 223-26, between the hermeneutical approach of Paul in 1 Cor 11:2-16 and that of the Vatican Declaration 'On the Question of the Admission of Women to the Ministerial Priesthood' (*Inter Insigniores*, [1976]).

3   Paul's respect for tradition is clear in even more central matters of the faith: the eucharistic *anamnêsis* (1 Cor 11:23), the resurrection creed (15:3-11), ethical instruction (Rom 6:17).

4   I find very impressive in this respect the firm opinion of Raymond Brown 'that little is gained in public reading by omitting offensive Bible passages, for bowdlerized versions permit people too easily to say they 'accept' the Bible. They never hear passages that should cause an intelligent audience to demur and ask themselves constructive questions that will lead them to recognize the human conditioning in the biblical account . . . to the realization that every word spoken about God on this earth, including the biblical word, . . . is a partial and limited witness to the truth' (*The Churches the Apostles Left Behind* 44; see earlier, *The Critical Meaning of the Bible* [New York: Paulist, 1981] 1-22). A recent article by J. Y. Thériault, 'La femme chrêtienne dans les textes pauliniens', ScEs 37 (1985) 297-317, has become available to me just as this present study is going to press. Particularly valuable and stimulating in the present context is the concluding series of hermeneutical reflections (pp. 310-17) on the 'reading' of the Pauline texts in present Church life.

Bibliography

Balch, D. L., *Let Wives Be Submissive: The Domestic Code in 1 Peter*, SBLMS 26; Chico, CA: Scholars, 1981.

Barrett, C. K., *The First Epistle to the Corinthians*, 2d ed; London: Black, 1971.

Barré, M. L., 'To marry or to burn', *CBQ* 36 (1974) 193-202.

Bartchy, S. Scott, *First Century Slavery and 1 Corinthians 7:21*, SBLDS 11; Missoula: SBL, 1974.

Barth, M., *Ephesians 4-6*, Anchor Bible 34 A; New York: Doubleday, 1979.

Beker, J. C., *Paul the Apostle*, Edinburgh: Clark, 1980.

Betz, H. D., *Galatians*, Hermeneia; Philadelphia: Fortress, 1979.

Boucher, M., 'Some Unexplored Parallels to 1 Cor 11:11-12 and Gal 3:28: The NT on the Role of Women', *CBQ* 31 (1969) 50-58.

Brooten, B., 'Junia . . . Outstanding among the Apostles', in L. and A. Swidler (eds.), *Woman Priests: A Catholic Commentary on the Vatican Declaration.* (New York: Paulist, 1977) 141-44.

——*Women Leaders in Ancient Synagogues*, Chico, CA: Scholars, 1982.

Brown, R., *The Critical Meaning of the Bible*, New York: Paulist, 1981.

——*The Churches the Apostles Left Behind*, New York: Paulist, 1984.

Byrne, B. J., *'Sons of God'* – *'Seed of Abraham',* Analecta Biblica 83; Rome: Biblical Institute Press, 1979.

——'Sinning against One's Own Body: Paul's Understanding of the Sexual Relationship in 1 Corinthians 6:18', *CBQ* 45 (1983) 608-16.

——'Eschatologies of Resurrection and Destruction: The Ethical Significance of Paul's Dispute with the Corinthians', *DR* 104 (1986) 288-98.

——*Reckoning with Romans*, Wilmington: Glazier, 1986.

Conzelmann, H., *1 Corinthians*, Hermeneia; Philadelphia: Fortress, 1975.

Cope, L., '1 Cor 11,2-16: One Step Further', *JBL* 97 (1978) 435-36.

Dalton, W. D., 'Pseudepigraphy in the New Testament', *Catholic Theological Review* (Melbourne) 5 (1983) 29-35.

Delling, G., Art. *'gnêsios'*, *TDNT* 1.748-50.

Delobel, J., '1 Cor 11,2-16: Towards a Coherent Interpretation', in A. Vanhoye (ed.) *L'Apôtre Paul* (BETL 73; Leuven: University Press, 1986) 369-98.

Dibelius, M. and Conzelmann, H., *The Pastoral Epistles*, Hermeneia; Philadelphia: Fortress, 1972.

Dungan, D., *The Sayings of Jesus in the Churches of Paul*, Oxford: Blackwell, 1971.

Evans, M., *Woman in the Bible*, Exeter: Paternoster, 1983.

Fàbrega, V., 'War Junia(s), der hervorragende Apostel (Rom 16,7), eine Frau?', *JahrAntChrist* 27-28 (1984-85) 47-64.

Feuillet, A., 'La dignité et le rôle de la femme d'après quelques textes pauliniens: comparaison avec l'Ancien Testament', *NTS* 21 (1975-76) 157-91.

Fiorenza, E. Schüssler, 'Women in the Pre-Pauline and Pauline Churches', *USQR* 33 (1978) 153-66.

——*In Memory of Her: A Feminist Theological Reconstruction of Christian Origins*, New York: Crossroad, 1983; London: SCM, 1983.

Fitzmyer, J. A., 'A Feature of Qumran Angelology and the Angels of 1 Cor 11:10' in *Essays on the Semitic Background of the New Testament* (London: Chapman, 1971) 187-204.

——'The Matthean Divorce Texts and Some New Palestinian Evidence', *TS* 37 (1976) 197-226.

Grassi, J. A., 'The Letter to the Ephesians' in *Jerome Biblical Commentary* 2.341-49.

Heine, S., *Women and Early Christianity*, London: SCM, 1987.

Hennecke, E., *New Testament Apocrypha*, Ed. W. Schneemelcher; 2 vols.; London: Lutterworth, 1963, 1965.

Hooker, M. D., 'Authority on her Head: An Examination of 1 Cor. xi. 10', *NTS* 10 (1963-64) 410-16.

Hurd, Jr., J. C., *The Origin of 1 Corinthians*, London: SPCK, 1965.

Hurley, J. B., 'Did Paul Require Veils or the Silence of Women? A Consideration of 1 Cor. 11:2-16 and 1 Cor. 14:33b-36', *WTJ* 35 (1973) 190-220.

Jaubert, A., 'Le Voile des femmes (1 Cor. xi. 2-16)', *NTS* 18 (1971-72) 419-30.

Jeremias, J., 'War Paulus Witwer?', *ZNW* 25 (1926) 310-12.

——'Nochmals: War Paulus Witwer?', *ZNW* 28 (1929) 321-23 (a response to a critique of the first article by E. Fascher, ibid. 62-69).

Jewett, R., 'The Sexual Liberation of the Apostle Paul', *JAAR* (Supplement) 47/1 (1979) 55-87.

Käsemann, E., 'Ministry and Community in the New Testament' in *Essays on New Testament Themes* (London: SCM, 1964) 63-94.

Kelly, J. N. D., *The Pastoral Epistles*, London: Black, 1963.

Kiley, M., *Colossians as Pseudepigraphy*, Sheffield: JSOT, 1986.

Kraemer, R. S., 'Women in the Religions of the Greco-Roman World', *RSR* 9 (1983) 127-39

Kümmel, W. G., *Introduction to the New Testament*, Rev. ed.; London: SCM, 1975.

Kürzinger, J., 'Frau und Mann nach 1 Kor 11,11f', *BZ* NF 22 (1978) 270-75.

Lagrange, M.-J., *Saint Paul: Epître aux Romains*, Paris: Gabalda, 1915, repr. with additions 1950.

Lösch, S., 'Christliche Frauen in Korinth (1 Kor 11, 2-16)', *TQ* 127 (1947) 216-61.

MacDonald, D. R., *There is No Male and Female*, HDR 20; Philadelphia: Fortress, 1986.

Malinowski, F. X., 'The Brave Women of Philippi', *BTB* 15 (1985) 60-64.

Meeks, W. A., 'The Image of the Androgyne', *HR* 13 (1974) 165-208.

——*The First Urban Christians*, New Haven: Yale University, 1983.

Meier, J. P., 'On the Veiling of Hermeneutics (1 Cor 11:2-16)', *CBQ* 40 (1978) 212-26.

Menoud, P. H., 'Marriage and Celibacy according to St. Paul', in *Jesus Christ and the Faith: a Collection of Studies* (Pittsburgh: Pickwick, 1978) 1-18.

Moloney, F. J., 'Matthew 19, 3-13 and Celibacy. A Form Critical and Redactional Study', *JSNT* 2 (1979) 42-60.

——*Disciples and Prophets*, London: Darton, Longman and Todd, 1980.

——*Woman: First Among the Faithful*, Melbourne: Dove, 1984.

Murphy-O'Connor, J., 'The Non-Pauline Character of 1 Corinthians 11,2-16', *JBL* 95 (1976) 615-21.

——'Sex and Logic in 1 Corinthians 11, 2-16', *CBQ* 42 (1980) 482-500.

——'Interpolations in 1 Corinthians', *CBQ* 48 (1986) 81-94.

Odell-Scott, D. W., 'Let the Women Speak in the Church. An Egalitarian Interpretation of 1 Cor 14:33b-36', *BTB* 13 (1983) 90-93.

Padgett, A., 'Paul on Women in the Church: The Contradictions of Coiffure in 1 Corinthians 11.2-16', *JSNT* 20 (1984) 69-86.

——'Feminism in First Corinthians: A Dialogue with Elisabeth Schüssler Fiorenza', *EvQ* 58 (1986) 121-32.

Pagels, E. H., 'Paul and Women: A Response to Recent Discussion', *JAAR* 42 (1974) 543-49.

——*The Gnostic Gospels*, New York: Random House, 1979.

Perrin, N. and Duling, D. C., *The New Testament: An Introduction*, 2d ed.; New York, etc.: Harcourt, Brace, Jovanovich, 1982.

Ramsay, W., *The Cities of St. Paul*, London: Hodder & Stoughton, 1911.

Robertson, A. and Plummer, A., *The First Epistle of St. Paul to the Corinthians*, ICC; Edinburgh: Clark, 1911.

Sampley, J. P., *'And the Two shall become One Flesh': A Study of Traditions in Ephesians 5:21-33*, Cambridge: Cambridge University, 1971.

——*Pauline Partnership in Christ*, Philadelphia: Fortress, 1980.

Schillebeeckx, E., *Marriage: Secular Reality and Saving Mystery*, London: Sheed and Ward, 1965.

Scroggs, R., *The Last Adam*, Philadelphia: Fortress, 1966.

——'Paul and the Eschatological Woman', *JAAR* 40 (1972) 283-303.

——'Paul and the Eschatological Woman Revisited', *JAAR* 42 (1974) 532-37.

——Art. 'Woman in the NT' in *IDBSupp* 966-968.

Shoemaker, T. P., 'Unveiling of Equality: 1 Corinthians 11:2-16', *BTB* 17 (1987) 60-63.

Stendahl, K., *The Bible and the Role of Women*, Philadelphia: Fortress, 1966.

Theissen, G., *Psychological Aspects of Pauline Theology*, Edinburgh: Clark, 1987.

——*The Social Setting of Pauline Christianity*, Philadelphia: Fortress, 1982.

Thériault, J. -Y., 'La femme chrêtienne dans les textes pauliniens', *ScEs* 37 (1985) 297-317.

Thüsing, W., *Per Christum in Deum*, 2d ed.; Münster: Aschendorff, 1969.

Trompf, G. W., 'On Attitudes toward Women in Paul and Paulinist Literature', *CBQ* 42 (1980) 196-215.

van der Horst, P. W., *The Sentences of Pseudo-Phocylides with Introduction and Commentary*, SVTP 4; Leiden: Brill, 1978.

Walker, Jr. W. O., '1 Corinthians 11:2-16 and Paul's Views Regarding Women', *JBL* 94 (1975) 94-100.

——'The "Theology of Woman's Place" and the "Paulinist" Tradition', *Semeia* 28 (1983) 101-12.

——'The Burden of Proof in Identifying Interpolations in the Pauline Letters', *NTS* 33 (1987) 610-618.

Witherington, B., 'Rite and Rights for Women – Gal 3:28', *NTS* 27 (1981) 593-604.

Yarbrough, O. L., *Not Like the Gentiles: Marriage Rules in the Letters of Paul*, SBLDS 80; Atlanta: Scholars, 1985.

Index of Authors